P. T. Barnum

P. T. Barnum

The World's
Greatest Showman

ALICE FLEMING

Walker and Company
NEW YORK

The author would like to thank Robert S. Pelton,
curator of the Barnum Museum in Bridgeport, Connecticut, for his
generous assistance in helping compile the
illustrations for this biography.

First published in the United States of America in 1993
by Walker Publishing Company, Inc.

Published simultaneously in Canada by Thomas Allen & Son
Canada, Limited, Markham, Ontario

Library of Congress Cataloging-in-Publication Data
Fleming, Alice Mulcahey, 1928–
P. T. Barnum : the world's greatest showman / Alice Fleming.
p. cm.
Includes bibliographical references and index.
ISBN 0-8027-8234-5 (cloth) —ISBN 0-8027-8235-3 (lib. bdg.)
1. Barnum, P. T. (Phineas Taylor), 1810–1891—Juvenile literature.
2. Circus owners—United States—Biography—Juvenile literature.
I. Title
GV1811.B3F54   1993
338.7'617913'092—dc20
[B]   93-14720
CIP
AC

Printed in the United States of America

2 4 6 8 10 9 7 5 3 1

Contents

P. T. Barnum

A Connecticut Yankee
Learns His Craft

Mention P. T. Barnum and most people think of the circus. Actually, running a circus was the last of his many careers. But in a sense P. T. Barnum's whole life was a circus—a flashy, splashy, three-ring extravaganza filled with stunts and surprises, studded with superlatives, and bursting with legendary stars. There was Jenny Lind, Jumbo the Elephant, and a bouncy midget named General Tom Thumb, and in the center ring, seldom out of the spotlight, was the one and only great P. T. himself.

Phineas Taylor Barnum began life quietly enough. He was born on July 5, 1810 in Bethel, a small town on the outskirts of Danbury, Connecticut. As an adult, P. T.

1

Barnum was often involved in two or three businesses at a time. He may have acquired the habit from his father. Philo Barnum was a farmer, the proprietor of the village tavern, a keeper of horses and carriages for hire, and the owner of a local freight service.

Philo Barnum was a widower with five children when he married Irena Taylor, the daughter of one of Bethel's most prominent citizens. Their first son was named after Irena's father. It is not clear whether the Barnums didn't really like the name Phineas or whether they felt that one Phineas in the family was enough. Whatever the reason, Phineas Taylor Barnum was rarely called anything but Taylor or Tale as a boy. When he got older, he dropped both names and called himself P. T.

At the age of six, Taylor was sent to the district school, where he proved to be one of the brightest boys in the class. His two best subjects were English and arithmetic. He showed a talent for writing and he could calculate sums in his head with astonishing speed and accuracy. One of his teachers was so impressed with his abilities that he made a bet with a neighbor that Taylor Barnum could compute the precise number of feet in a load of wood in five minutes.

Eager to collect his winnings, the teacher appeared at the Barnums' house that very evening and dragged his pupil out of bed. Taylor obligingly tackled the problem and delighted his teacher by coming up with the correct answer in only two minutes.

Like most people in Connecticut in those days, the

Barnums were faithful churchgoers. Irena Barnum made sure her children knew the New Testament and the catechism. As a result, Taylor was also a prize pupil in his Sunday school class.

Any boy who lived on a farm was expected to do his share of chores—raking the hay, feeding the livestock, driving the cows back and forth to the pasture. Taylor hated them all. It wasn't that he objected to working. On the contrary, he enjoyed being busy. But he preferred to use his wits instead of his hands, and he also liked to get paid.

Taylor's interest in money began at an early age. He started saving pennies even before he went to school, and by the time he was six, he had accumulated enough coins to exchange for a silver dollar.

As he got older, he earned ten cents a day for riding the horse that led the ox team that plowed his father's fields. He also took his first crack at being a salesman. On training days, when the local militia turned out to drill, Taylor Barnum could be found on the town green selling molasses candy, gingerbread, and cherry rum to the hungry, thirsty men.

Being Phineas Taylor's grandson was something of a distinction. He owned quite a bit of property in Bethel and he was also known for his sense of humor. He was constantly telling funny stories and making witty remarks, but his favorite sport was playing practical jokes.

In his autobiography, P. T. Barnum described his grandfather as a man who would "go farther, wait longer, work harder and contrive deeper, to carry out a practical joke, than for anything else under heaven."

Taylor was the victim of one of those elaborate jokes. Beginning somewhere around his fourth birthday, Phineas Taylor regularly announced to the boy, and to everyone else in Bethel, that Taylor was the richest child in town. The source of his wealth was a five-acre tract of land known as Ivy Island that his grandfather had deeded to the boy when he was born. To hear the old man tell it, the property was the most valuable farm in Connecticut.

Everyone in Bethel, including Philo and Irena Barnum, regularly talked about Taylor's good fortune. They teasingly wondered if he would still speak to them when he grew up and took over his marvelous estate.

After eight years of hearing about Ivy Island, the boy was finally taken to see the place. The supposedly valuable farm turned out to be nothing but a weed-choked patch of land in the middle of a swamp. Its lone inhabitant was a large black snake that came slithering toward the disappointed landowner and sent him scrambling back to Bethel.

When Taylor reached home, he found his grandfather and all the members of his family, along with half the population of Bethel, gathered in front of the fireplace waiting to hear what he thought of his estate.

Then, not content with the sight of the twelve-year-old squirming and stammering with embarrassment, they refused to let the matter drop. As Barnum described it more than three decades later, the residents of Bethel, having spent eight years preparing for the joke, went on to spend the next five laughing about it.

It seems like a cruel trick to play on an unsuspecting boy, but if Barnum was bothered by it, he never let on. Perhaps even at that early age, he had developed the talent for sloughing off setbacks that was to stand him in good stead in his adult life.

As for his family and friends, they probably didn't think twice about the matter. Practical jokes were a common form of humor in the nineteenth century. Some of the better ones were actually reported in the newspapers. It was considered something of a triumph to pull off a clever prank, and the victim who complained was generally dismissed as a sore loser.

After learning everything he could at the district school, Taylor Barnum went on to study at the Danbury Academy. Academies were private schools similar to today's high schools. Some of the boys at the Academy had plans for college, but Taylor was not among them. He left school some time before his sixteenth birthday and went to work as a clerk in the general store his father and a partner had opened in Bethel.

The experience taught him lessons he never learned in school. New Englanders in general, and the citizens of Connecticut in particular, had a reputation for sharp trading. The state supposedly got its nickname, the Nutmeg State, because its peddlers were notorious for selling wooden nutmegs to unwary customers.

Taylor found himself up against some similar Yankee tricks. The store operated mainly on the barter system, with the local farmers trading their goods for whatever they needed from his stock. A customer would often bring in a sack of corn or oats that turned out to be several bushels less than he claimed. Just as often, a bundle that supposedly contained linen and cotton rags to be resold to make paper would be half-full of cheaper scraps.

Connecticut Yankees didn't consider such practices dishonest. They viewed almost every business transaction as a contest, a matter of outwitting an opponent by getting the better of him in a bargain.

About two months after Taylor Barnum's sixteenth birthday, his father died. The tragedy was compounded by the fact that Philo Barnum left a great many debts and most of his property had to be auctioned off to pay them. Under Connecticut law, however, Irena Barnum was allowed to keep the family farm. She also took over the management of the village tavern and was thus able to support herself and her younger children. There was no need to worry about her oldest son. He was already supporting himself.

Although Taylor enjoyed his job in the general store, the salary was small and there was no opportunity to make any extra money on the side. He eventually left to clerk in a similar store about a mile away in the town of Grassy Plain. The owners of the new place didn't mind if he spun off a few business ventures of his own, and they were willing to let him keep whatever money he made from them.

Taylor spotted his first chance to make a private profit when a man appeared at the store with a wagon-load of green glass bottles. The enterprising young clerk offered to take them in exchange for some merchandise that his employers had never been able to sell. He congratulated himself on getting rid of the worthless stuff, but now he was stuck with another problem. How was he going to get rid of the equally worthless green glass bottles? It didn't take Taylor long to come up with the answer. He'd raffle them off in a lottery.

The drawing was announced with a splash. Boldly lettered posters appeared on fence posts and barns, and handbills were distributed all over town. The tickets were amazingly cheap, and best of all, there were over six hundred prizes—enough to produce more winners than losers.

The listing of the prizes made no mention of green glass bottles. In fact, it was carefully worded to avoid naming specific prizes and to direct the ticket buyers' attention to the amounts of money at stake instead. The grand prize winner would be allowed to select twenty-five dollars' worth of any goods in the store. The next hundred winners would receive prizes worth five dollars each, the next hundred, prizes worth one dollar each, the next hundred, prizes worth fifty cents each, and the final three hundred, prizes worth twenty-five cents each.

The lottery sounded like such a foolproof proposition that in their haste to buy tickets, the participants also failed to notice that all but the grand prize were to be selected not by the winners, but by the lottery's sponsor.

When the drawing was over, the grand prize winner carried off some valuable items, but the other winners found themselves carting home various quantities of green bottles along with some battered tin plates and cups that had been lying around the store for years.

Taylor Barnum made a tidy profit on the lottery. He also won the gratitude of his employers for disposing of two large lots of unsalable goods. The prize winners may have been chagrined and disappointed, but none of them complained. They had gotten exactly what they were promised. No harm had been done, and the lottery had brought some temporary excitement into their otherwise humdrum lives.

From Bethel to the Big City

When he was eleven years old, Taylor Barnum made a brief visit to New York City. He earned a few dollars helping a cattle drover drive a herd of cattle to market. Taylor was fascinated by the bustle and excitement of the big city and wanted to see more of it, but it was five years before he returned. One of his relatives, Oliver Taylor, offered him a job in his Brooklyn grocery store when Taylor was sixteen, and he quickly accepted.

At that time Brooklyn was a separate city, but it was right across the East River from New York and Taylor regularly took the ferry back and forth. Oliver Taylor had entrusted him with the job of purchasing the goods for his store. This required him to spend much of his time in lower Manhattan searching out bargains in tea, sugar, molasses, and other foods.

Taylor became an expert at making deals with the wholesale merchants, but eventually he got tired of the job. The pay was only so-so, and although he enjoyed using his wits, he was unhappy with the fact that he was using them for his boss's benefit, not his own.

A bout of smallpox forced him to take a leave of absence from the grocery business. When he recovered several months later, he gave Oliver Taylor his notice and invested his small savings in a Brooklyn porterhouse. Porter is a type of dark beer or stout, but porterhouses also sold other types of alcoholic beverages.

Business was good, and after a few months Taylor sold the place at a profit and took a job as a clerk at another porterhouse in New York City. The establishment was a popular gathering place for the hatters and comb makers from Danbury and Bethel who came to New York on business, so he was constantly running into people from home.

Within a year, however, Taylor returned to Bethel. His grandfather, Phineas Taylor, had offered him half of a carriage house he owned near the center of town. It was an ideal spot to set up some type of business, and Taylor could have it rent-free. The offer was too good to turn down, but Taylor had another reason for wanting to go home.

While he was clerking in Grassy Plain, he had met an attractive young woman named Chairy—short for Charity—Hallett. She lived in Bethel but had ridden up to Grassy Plain one Saturday afternoon to buy a new

Charity Hallett Barnum as she appeared in her middle age. Despite her stern appearance, Charity had a lively sense of humor and won her husband's admiration for her quick comebacks to his jokes. (*Courtesy of Barnum Museum, Bridgeport, Connecticut*)

bonnet and been caught in a violent thunderstorm along the way. The storm was still raging when she was ready to go home, and she was nervous about making the trip alone.

The woman who sold her the bonnet knew that Taylor Barnum boarded with a family in Grassy Plain during the week but returned to Bethel on Saturday evenings to spend Sundays with his family. She sent him a message asking if he would be returning to Bethel as usual that evening, and if so, would he escort Charity Hallett home.

The answer was yes, and an hour or so later Taylor found himself riding home beside a fair-haired young woman with rosy cheeks and beautiful white teeth. She was such a pleasant traveling companion that he began to wish that Bethel was twenty miles away instead of only one.

Taylor said good-bye to Chairy at her doorstep, but he saw her again in church the next day. Before long, Chairy and Taylor were seeing each other every chance they got. In the summer of 1829, a little over a year after his return to Bethel, Taylor asked Chairy to marry him. She readily agreed, but because Irena Barnum was not enthusiastic about the match, they decided to keep their engagement a secret.

Some months later, Chairy went to New York City to visit her uncle, Nathan Beers. Not long after that, Taylor went to New York on what he claimed was a business trip. On November 8, the couple were married in

Nathan Beers's parlor. They returned to Bethel a few days later and took rooms in the boardinghouse where Chairy had been living before her marriage.

As agreed, Taylor opened a shop in one half of his grandfather's carriage house. He sold fancy foods such as fruit, candy, and oysters, along with pocketbooks, jewelry, combs, and toys. His profits were good, but Phineas Taylor, anxious to see his grandson succeed, knew the way to make them better. He advised Taylor to set up an agency to sell lottery tickets on commission.

Lotteries were a booming business in those days. Anyone could set one up, and there were hundreds of them operating all over the country with cash prizes that totaled millions of dollars each year. Taylor became an agent for several of the larger lotteries. He received a commission for every ticket he sold, so naturally he wanted to sell as many as he could.

As part of his sales strategy, he called his agency the Temple of Fortune and filled its windows with immense gold signs holding out the promise of instant wealth. The signs were printed in brightly colored ink with bold lettering and plenty of exclamation points. He also launched an advertising campaign, deluging Bethel with handbills and circulars and taking out full-page ads in the local newspaper. His repeated claim was that the Temple of Fortune had more winners in every lottery than any other office in the country.

Ticket sales were so brisk that Taylor opened up smaller agencies in the villages around Bethel and set up branch offices in Danbury, Norwalk, Stamford, and Middletown. On a good day, he sold as much as $2,000 worth of lottery tickets. Even when business was slow, the figure seldom went below $500.

Taylor used his sudden wealth to buy a piece of property and build a new house for himself and Charity along with a new and much larger general store. The store was not as successful as he had hoped—or perhaps he had simply become impatient with making money the slow way. In any event, he sold the store within a few months and set out in a completely different direction, newspaper editing. He bought his own printing press and started a four-page weekly called *Herald of Freedom*. The paper never made much money, but with his lottery business to support him, Barnum didn't care. It gave him a chance to present his opinions on two highly controversial topics—religion and politics.

In Connecticut, the two were closely related. The major political parties of the era, the Federalists and the Jeffersonian Democrats, were sharply divided along religious lines. The Federalists were almost all Congregationalists, while the more liberal Jeffersonian Democrats tended to attract the Universalists.

As a boy, Taylor had attended the Congregational Church. At the time, it was the only one in Bethel and Congregationalism was the official religion in Connecticut. He believed in God but was terrified by the stern, frowning, fire-and-brimstone deity of the Congregationalists.

By the time he reached his teens, other denominations had founded churches in the state. Once they had a choice, he and his family joined the Universalists. The Universalists' God appealed to Taylor because He was more benevolent and forgiving. His mission was not to consign sinners to hell, but to bring holiness and happiness to all mankind.

As a staunch member of the Universalist Church, Barnum was also a staunch Democrat. The *Herald of Freedom* took a strong stand on one of the party's favorite issues—the need for strict separation between church and state.

This was a thorny subject in Connecticut. Congregationalism had ceased being the state's official religion in 1818, but its clergy still had a strong say in who was nominated for public office. This provided the Democrats with their best argument for booting the Federalists out of office.

The *Herald of Freedom* mounted a fierce campaign against the Federalists, attacking their private lives as well as their political views. As a result, its editor became a target of their wrath. They scrutinized every issue of his paper, hoping to find some false and malicious statement that would give them grounds to sue him for libel. Since Taylor Barnum never let the truth stand in the way of a good story, they found plenty of reasons to haul him into court.

He was involved in three libel suits in three years. He managed to get acquitted in the first trial but was found guilty in the second and forced to pay $215 in fines. In the third trial, he was found guilty again. This time the judge gave him the choice of paying a fine or being sentenced to jail for sixty days. Barnum chose jail, guessing—correctly—that it would be a good way to win public sympathy.

His stay in the Danbury jail proved to be more of a vacation than a punishment. His cell was clean and well-furnished, and visitors could drop by whenever they pleased. The jail term also turned out to be a smart business move. In the aftermath of his sentencing, the *Herald of Freedom* gained several hundred new subscribers.

The most important result of the episode, however, was that it gave Taylor Barnum his first taste of the lime-light. At the appointed hour of his release, a crowd of Democrats gathered on the Danbury town green, raised the flag, and fired a salute. There were speeches praising the twenty-two-year-old editor as a martyr for two fundamental American rights—freedom of religion and freedom of the press.

That evening a banquet was given in his honor. He was treated to another round of complimentary speeches, and toasts were drunk in his honor. At the end of it all, Taylor Barnum was driven home in a coach drawn by six horses, the chief attraction in a boisterous parade that included forty horsemen, sixty carriages, and a brass band.

P. T. Barnum basked in his new celebrity. It won him the friendship of Connecticut's Democratic politicians, and he made frequent trips to Hartford, the state capital, to hobnob with party leaders. There were good things happening at home, too. In the spring of 1833, Charity gave birth to their first child, a little girl whom they named Caroline Cordelia.

But Taylor Barnum's future was far from bright. On the contrary, it was looking more and more uncertain. The Temple of Fortune, which had made him a very prosperous young man, would soon be a thing of the past.

The lottery business had degenerated into a public nuisance. There were problems with counterfeit tickets, rigged drawings, and managers who stole the jackpots. Social reformers were also becoming concerned about the lower classes gambling away their wages, leaving their families with nothing to live on.

Starting in the early 1830s, a number of states voted to outlaw lotteries. In 1834, Connecticut followed suit. The Temple of Fortune closed down and Taylor Barnum was forced to seek another line of work.

He had already exhausted the opportunities in Bethel; he needed a bigger world to conquer. Toward the end of the year, he turned over the editorship of the *Herald of Freedom* to his sister's husband and he and Charity and their baby daughter moved to New York.

The Search for the Right Opportunity

P. T. Barnum wasn't sure exactly what he was going to do in New York. He had a family to support, so he needed a job with a regular salary. At the same time, he wanted the sense of accomplishment—and the profits—that would come from running his own business.

Since he couldn't afford to wait for the ideal opportunity, he took the first job that came along, drumming up business for a store that sold men's neckwear and hats. It suited his talents—he had always been good at persuading people to buy things—but it was menial work for a man who had managed his own store. P. T. wasn't proud. It would do until something better turned up.

Barnum spent his spare time poring over the ads in the newspapers looking for a better business to get into.

The only offer that appealed to him was from a man who wanted to sell a new type of microscope that was currently being exhibited at Scudder's American Museum. The ad promised that the microscope would bring in $10,000 a year from being displayed in theaters, museums, and lecture halls around the country.

Exhibits of one sort or another were a popular form of entertainment in those days. There was a shortage of ready-made amusements, and people would gladly pay to see something—almost anything—they hadn't seen before. As long as he could keep the public interested, a man who owned an unusual exhibit had a guaranteed income.

P. T. would have liked to get into the exhibit business, but the asking price for the microscope—$2,000—made it out of the question. Instead, he bought a small boardinghouse on Frankfort Street in lower Manhattan. It provided him with a decent income, but since Charity saw to the housekeeping, it left him with little to do. To keep from getting bored, he took part of the profits from the boardinghouse and bought a half interest in a grocery store.

One day while P. T. was tending shop in the store, an old friend from Connecticut dropped by. In the course of their conversation, the man happened to mention that a friend of his was trying to sell his interest in an exhibit.

This exhibit was not a scientific curiosity like the microscope, but a human one—a blind, black slave

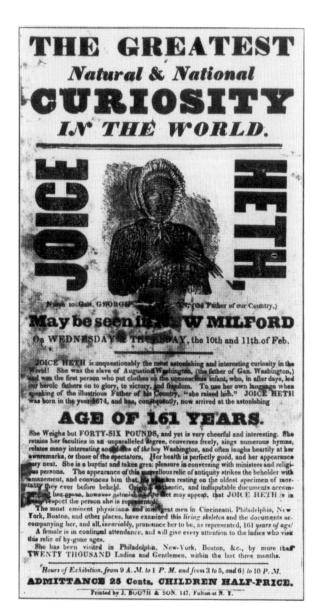

A handbill advertising one of Joice Heth's last performances. She appeared in New Milford, Connecticut, on February 10 and 11, 1836, and died in Bethel on February 19. *(Courtesy of Historical Collections, Bridgeport Public Library)*

woman named Joice Heth who claimed to be 161 years old. As if that wasn't amazing enough, she also claimed to have been owned by George Washington's father, Augustine, and to have been our first president's childhood nurse.

P. T. Barnum was practically counting the money he could make from this extraordinary exhibit. He was so excited by the prospect that he went rushing off to Philadelphia, where Joice Heth's current owner was exhibiting her at the Masonic Hall.

Barnum was impressed by what he saw. The woman looked every bit as ancient as she claimed. She was wrinkled and shrunken, she had no teeth, and her legs were so withered they could not carry her weight. She spoke to her audiences while reclining on a couch.

In spite of her decrepit appearance, the old woman's mind was clear and her voice was strong enough to be heard throughout the hall. She could hold a crowd spellbound with her stories about "dear little George" and her reminiscences about life in colonial Virginia. She made it all sound very convincing, but to allay any suspicions and establish her credentials as an honest, God-fearing woman, she concluded her act by singing a few hymns and describing her baptism in the Potomac River in 1719.

As far as P. T. Barnum was concerned, the commercial possibilities of managing Joice Heth were too good to pass up. He talked the man who was exhibiting her into dropping his asking price from $3,000 to $1,000.

Then he returned to New York, sold his interest in the grocery store, and hurried back to Philadelphia to collect his exhibit and begin his career as a showman.

Barnum had already found a hall for Joice Heth to appear in. Instead of letting people stand and stare at her as they had done in Philadelphia, however, he organized a program, hiring a former lawyer named Levi Lyman to introduce her to the audience and answer any questions they might have. This gave the performance an educational tone. The country was still beset by puritanical attitudes, and many people who would not pay for mere entertainment would gladly patronize exhibits that claimed to be instructive.

As part of the exhibit, Levi Lyman was also given a tattered, faded bill of sale to display to the audience. Dated February 5, 1727, it was for a fifty-four-year-old Negro slave named Joice Heth and the signature read "Augustine Washington."

Barnum's next step was to flood New York with handbills and newspaper ads. As he remarked some years later, "What's a show without notoriety?"

He knew it was essential to arouse people's curiosity, to get them so interested and excited about Joice Heth that they simply had to come see her. Between his talent for writing and his taste for exaggeration, this was hardly a challenge.

Hundreds of people showed up to see the "rare spectacle." They were not disappointed. Joice Heth gave them good value for their money. She had a fund of interesting and entertaining stories, including her experiences with the Redcoats during the American Revolution.

When business began to slow down in New York, Barnum sent Joice Heth on a tour through New England. The antislavery movement was already underway in that part of the country, so he was careful not to let on that Joice was the property of a Kentucky man who leased her out to exhibitors.

While he never actually said that Joice was free, he did everything possible to give that impression. He planted a story in a Providence, Rhode Island, newspaper that described Joice Heth as the mother of fifteen children, the youngest of whom had recently died at the age of 116. The story also said that she planned to use the proceeds of her performances to buy freedom for her five great-grandchildren, who lived in slavery in Kentucky.

About six months after Barnum started exhibiting Joice Heth, she became seriously ill. She was making her second tour through New England at the time, and he arranged for her to be taken to Bethel, where she was cared for in the home of his half brother, Philo. Joice Heth did not recover from her illness. After her death, a New York doctor, who had apparently fallen for the story of her advanced age, requested permission to perform an autopsy as a matter of scientific interest. His findings should not have surprised anyone with an ounce of common sense: The supposedly 161-year-old woman wasn't a day over eighty.

When the autopsy report was made public, P. T. Barnum was denounced as a humbug. He flatly denied the charge, insisting that the real humbug was Joice Heth's previous manager, who had hoodwinked him into believing her tales.

A decade later, however, Barnum admitted to a friend that he had known the truth all along. Not only had he written Joice Heth's script and rehearsed her in her lines, he had also forged the bill of sale with Augustine Washington's signature on it and treated the paper to make it look old.

Joice Heth, of course, was a willing accomplice to the deception. Barnum took very good care of her, and she enjoyed being a star. It was infinitely better than spending her declining years as a crippled old slave on her master's plantation.

Even before the furor over Joice Heth died down, Barnum signed up another exhibit—an Italian juggler named Signor Antonio who billed himself as a "professor of equilibrium and plate dancing." Among his other feats, the professor could keep eight or ten plates dancing waltzes and minuets on the ends of sticks, which he sometimes held in his hands and sometimes balanced on his nose or chin.

Signor Antonio's juggling was definitely above average, but Barnum decided that a little hype wouldn't hurt. He changed the man's name to Signor Vivalla and advertised him as "Just Arrived from Italy"—a blatant lie, since Barnum had discovered him in Albany, New York. Unbothered by such a minor detail, Barnum advertised the professor's engagement at the Franklin Theater in New York as his first American appearance.

After a successful run in New York, Barnum took his new exhibit on tour to Boston, Washington, and Philadelphia. Things went well in Boston and Washington, but in Philadelphia, the turnout was distressingly small. Groping for a way to fill the house, Barnum found it one evening when the juggler's act drew a hostile hiss from someone in the audience.

The hisser turned out to be a rival juggler named J. B. Roberts. When Barnum asked him what he disliked about Signor Vivalla's performance, he announced with a sneer that he could do everything the Italian did and more. Barnum saw his chance. He issued a public announcement that Signor Vivalla was offering a prize of $1,000 to any performer who could duplicate his feats.

Roberts accepted the challenge, but when Barnum called on him to discuss the details of the match, his bravado had faded and he was ready to back out. Barnum was willing to do almost anything to salvage his publicity stunt. Discovering that Roberts was unemployed, he offered to pay him to appear with Signor Vivalla. Barnum would then play up the contest as a major event in juggling history. Unknown to the public, however, the supposed archrivals would rehearse their tricks to make sure they put on a convincing show.

Barnum advertised the event all over Philadelphia, and on the appointed night the Walnut Street Theater was packed with ticket buyers. As planned, Vivalla won the contest, but also as planned, Roberts immediately demanded a rematch, thus assuring Barnum of another huge turnout for his show. The gimmick was so successful that Barnum cooked up a similar competition when Signor Vivalla returned to New York.

By now, P. T. was making enough money in show business to allow the Barnums to give up their boardinghouse. He had also sampled enough of the business to know that he liked it. When Signor Vivalla's audiences began to decline, he signed a contract for a six-month tour with the Old Columbian Circus, which was owned by a Danbury man named Aaron Turner. Barnum's job was to sell tickets and keep the books, and Vivalla became part of the troupe.

The Old Columbian Circus was really no more than a small wagon show. Its principal stars, in addition to Signor Vivalla, were Turner's two sons, who did stunts on horseback, and the multitalented Joe Pentland, who was a combination magician, ventriloquist, and clown.

The circus left Danbury every spring and made a six-month circuit of New England and the Middle Atlantic States, then south to Virginia and North Carolina. The traveling was slow and uncomfortable, but Barnum and Aaron Turner managed to liven up the trip by playing practical jokes on each other. One of Turner's pranks almost cost Barnum his life.

During a stop in Annapolis, Maryland, Turner spotted his ticket seller wearing a new black suit. He pointed him out to a group of townspeople as the Reverend Ephraim K. Avery, a Rhode Island clergyman who had been tried and acquitted in a sensational murder case that made headlines all over the country. It was generally agreed that Avery had been guilty, and Turner expressed surprise that the good people of Annapolis would tolerate him in their town.

His remarks triggered a near-riot. In no time at all, a mob gathered. They seized Barnum, bombarded him with insults, and were threatening to lynch him. It took a lot of fast talking to persuade their leaders to take him to Aaron Turner, who cheerfully admitted that he had made up the story as a joke.

Barnum concluded his six-month tour with Aaron Turner at the end of October 1836. The Old Columbian Circus was in Warrenton, North Carolina, at the time. Instead of going home to Bethel, where Charity and little Caroline were living during his absence, Barnum decided to put together his own variety show, "Barnum's Grand Scientific and Musical Theater," and spend the winter touring the South.

The show featured Signor Vivalla, Joe Pentland, and a black singer named Robert White. It did well enough in the rural South, but the performers would have been booed off the stage in more sophisticated parts of the country. When Robert White abruptly left the show, for instance, Barnum blackened his face and performed in his stead. On another occasion, Barnum was bitten by a squirrel while assisting Joe Pentland in his magic act. Jolted by the pain and shock, he upset the table Pentland was using and completely ruined his trick.

"Barnum's Grand Scientific and Musical Theater" managed to survive because most of its patrons had never seen a show before. Not only did they not know the difference between a good performance and a bad one, they had a hard time understanding much of what was going on.

At the close of one performance, Joe Pentland stepped forward and announced: "Ladies and gentlemen, the entertainments of the evening have now come to a conclusion and, we hope, to your general satisfaction."

His listeners remained in their seats, thinking he had announced an upcoming act. Next Signor Vivalla gave it a try. His statement was very much to the point: "It is finished." But the audience had never heard an Italian accent before, so, again, the message failed to get through.

As they sat there refusing to budge, Vivalla became irritated and pulled down the curtain on the makeshift stage. Unfortunately, this only further convinced the audience that a new act was about to begin.

Finally, P. T. Barnum stepped out on the stage. "It is all over," he told the crowd, gesturing for them to leave. "No more performance. The show is out." Only then did the disappointed spectators rise from their seats and begin filing out.

By the time Barnum's variety show disbanded in Nashville the following May, its manager was more than ready to go home. He missed Charity and little Caroline, and he was sick of traveling from town to town, living in cheap hotels, and eating terrible food. He was also sick of being looked down on by respectable people who had no use for traveling shows or the people connected with them.

He still liked show business and he thought he could succeed at it, but being a traveling showman was the bottom of the ladder. P. T. Barnum had his eye on the top.

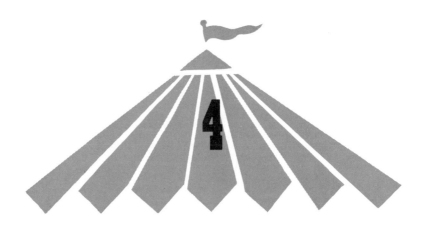

Opportunity Knocks at Last

On the trip back to New York, P. T. Barnum made two promises to himself: He was going to find a more respectable line of work, and he was never going on the road again. As it turned out, neither was easy to keep.

He began his search for a new occupation by placing an ad in one of the New York newspapers stating that he had $2,500 to invest and was looking for a good business opportunity. There was no shortage of responses, but most of the offers sounded either illegal or insane. The only one worthy of serious consideration came from a German named Proler who manufactured cologne, shoe polish, and a product called bear's grease, which supposedly cured baldness.

Barnum went to see Proler and found him to be a pleasant man who gave every indication of being honest and dependable. He had manufacturing plants in several major cities and needed a partner to keep the accounts and tend to sales in his New York store.

The business appeared to be thriving, and Barnum agreed to become Proler's partner. For the first few months, everything went well. Then some large bills that Proler had neglected to mention came due and there was not enough money in the accounts to pay them. At that point, Proler abruptly announced that he had to return to Europe. He dissolved the partnership and gave Barnum a note for $2,600 for his share of the business. Proler was halfway across the Atlantic before Barnum discovered that his former partner was deeply in debt and the note was worthless.

Luckily, Barnum had another iron in the fire. Reluctant to give up show business completely, he had contracted for the services of Master Jack Diamond, a black teenager. Master Diamond was one of the first and best of a number of performers who entertained the country during the nineteenth century with a specialty called Ethiopian breakdown dancing. The routines involved the dancers twisting their feet and legs in seemingly impossible directions and executing all sorts of tricky steps. While Barnum was working with Proler, Master Diamond was touring the country with an agent and Barnum was pocketing a share of his receipts.

In the spring of 1840, Charity gave birth to the Barnums' second daugher, Helen, and in an effort to support his growing family, P. T. returned to show business full-time. He assembled a variety show and booked it into New York's Vauxhall Garden, a combination saloon and theater that was much like today's nightclubs.

The show was a flop, and Barnum, desperate for money, decided to go on the road again. He put together a company of performers headed by Master Jack Diamond and set off on a tour that took them to Buffalo, Toronto, Detroit, Chicago, Ottawa, Springfield, St. Louis, and New Orleans.

When he returned home eight months later, he was richer than he had been when he left, but he was also more disgusted than ever with the life of a traveling showman. There had to be a better way to make a living, and P. T. Barnum was determined to find it.

The business he chose seemed like a natural for a man with a gift for salesmanship and a love of religion. He obtained the rights to sell a book of illustrated Bible stories and set up branch offices around the country.

Despite all his vows to the contrary, he could not resist taking another crack at show business. He put together another variety show and booked it into the Vauxhall Garden. Fearful of jeopardizing his reputation as a seller of religious books, however, he had Charity's brother lease the theater and represent him in the business dealings.

The show was an even bigger flop than his previous presentation at Vauxhall Garden. After three months of performances, it netted a measly $200. The illustrated Bible business, which had once seemed like such a sure thing, was not doing much better. Barnum and his agents sold thousands of copies, but there were scarcely any profits. Dishonest agents in the branch offices were skimming them off.

Within the space of a few months, P. T. Barnum's income spiraled steadily downward until he was, as he described it in his autobiography, "about as poor as I should ever wish to be."

It was a difficult time for the Barnums, but P. T. was not the type to sit around feeling sorry for himself. Instead he turned to his talent for writing. He sold a few articles to the Sunday newspapers and found a steady job writing advertisements for the Bowery Amphitheatre, a privately owned Zoological Institute that had an impressive menagerie, including an elephant, lions, tigers, and a llama. The job paid four dollars a week, and in addition to writing the ads, Barnum was expected to deliver them to the newspapers and make sure they were properly printed.

At this stage of his life, Phineas Taylor Barnum looked like a man without much future. He had invested in two separate businesses and both had failed. He had experienced some brief success as a showman but eventually he had failed at that too. He was thirty years old, he had a wife and two small daughters to support, and he was barely making a living.

The world may have looked bleak, but P. T. Barnum was an incurable optimist. He knew that the right opportunity was out there somewhere and that it was only a matter of time before he found it.

One day in the summer of 1841, Barnum was in his office at the Bowery Amphitheatre when a fellow employee happened to mention that Scudder's American Museum was for sale. Barnum's eyes lit up. This was the opportunity he had been looking for. One way or another, he was going to buy it.

The idea of buying a museum sounds odd today when practically all museums are public institutions, but in the first half of the nineteenth century, America's museums, zoos, aquariums, and botanical gardens were all privately owned.

These early museums had wide-ranging collections. The painter Charles Willson Peale founded the first one in Philadelphia in 1784 to display his portraits of famous Americans. Since Peale was also interested in nature and science, he added stuffed birds and animals, Indian artifacts, and specimens of plant life and minerals, along with some items from the Lewis and Clark Expedition donated by Thomas Jefferson. Although Peale operated his museum for a profit, it had an aura of being maintained strictly for the public good. This impression was reinforced by the fact that he numbered distinguished Americans like James Madison and Alexander Hamilton among his sponsors and supporters.

Peale's success prompted the founding of similar establishments in other cities. Many of them offered scholarly lectures along with their exhibits. As time went on, however, the number of people who were interested in such high-minded pursuits began to decline. If the museums wanted to stay in business, they had to find some livelier attractions.

Their lecture halls, which were actually small theaters, gradually became the setting for concerts, plays, and magic lantern shows. The art and science exhibits were supplemented with collections of curiosities and oddities whose chief value was that the public would pay to see them. Peale's Museum, for example, eventually added wax dummies, a chip of wood from the British coronation chair in Westminster Abbey, the tattooed head of a New Zealand aborigine chief, and a cow with five legs and two tails.

While museums still retained their standing as centers of science and culture, they also had their feet firmly planted in the entertainment business. For P. T. Barnum, it was a perfect combination. He could be respectable and a showman at the same time, and with any luck, he could get rich in the bargain.

The museum that Barnum had his heart set on buying had been founded by John Scudder, a taxidermist and student of natural history. For many years, it had been the finest in New York. It contained historical relics and curiosities donated by people from all over the country. Some of the more exotic objects had been collected by sea captains on their voyages to Africa, South America, and the Orient.

There were showcases full of stuffed animals, fossils, and mineral specimens; exhibits of new and unusual tools and machines; miniature models of Paris, Dublin, and Jerusalem; and a zoo that included lions and tigers, an anaconda, an orangutan, and an alligator.

After Scudder's death, a board of trustees was appointed to run the museum for the benefit of his daughters. For a while, they did a good job, adding to the collections and moving them into a five-story building, at Broadway and Ann Street in New York City, that had been designed to their specifications.

Eventually, however, the American Museum fell on hard times. The combination of a financial panic and competition from the rival New York Museum caused a decline in revenues. There was not enough money to add to the collections, nobody took the trouble to book entertaining programs into the Lecture Room, and business gradually fell off.

Barnum was convinced that with a few new exhibits, some better attractions in the Lecture Room, and a great deal of advertising and publicity, the American Museum could return to its former prominence. He was also convinced that he was the perfect man for the job. Perfect, that is, except for one thing. He didn't have the money to buy the museum.

One of P. T.'s friends put it to him bluntly when he told him of his plans. "You buy the American Museum!" he said. "What do you intend buying it with?"

Barnum conceded that he had no gold or silver

coins, but he had an ample supply of another metal—brass—and he planned to use it.

The building in which Scudder's Museum was housed was rented from a man named Francis Olmsted. Barnum wrote him a letter informing him that he wanted to buy the museum and felt certain he could turn it into a profitable enterprise within a fairly short time. Since he did not have the purchase price, he asked Mr. Olmsted to buy it for him and allow Barnum to pay him back in weekly installments.

After interviewing Barnum and checking out his references, Olmsted agreed to the proposal. Barnum next met with John Heath, the administrator of John Scudder's estate who managed the museum for his daughters. The asking price for the collection of objects that comprised the museum was $15,000. Barnum persuaded Heath to reduce it to $12,000. He returned to Olmsted, who agreed to lend him the sum, and the matter appeared to be settled.

Before the contract could be signed, however, Heath abruptly announced that he had a better offer. The directors of the New York Museum were willing to pay the original price of $15,000. They had already put down a deposit of $1,000 and agreed to pay the balance by December 26 of that year.

Barnum was stunned. Hadn't he and Heath already reached an agreement? Not at all, said the administrator. There was nothing in writing. Besides, he had an obligation to get the best possible price for John Scudder's heirs.

P. T. Barnum refused to give up. He knew that the New York Museum was almost as faded as Scudder's and probably had about the same number of patrons. Why would its directors want to take on another museum when there was a good chance they were losing money on the one they already had?

Barnum started asking a few questions about the prospective purchasers, and the more questions he asked, the more convinced he became that something crooked was going on. Not one of the directors of the New York Museum Company had any experience in museum management. They had bought the establishment for a pittance a few months earlier with the idea of turning a quick profit on it.

After further digging, Barnum discovered that their plan was to announce a merger of the two museums and sell stock in the company that would manage them. The price of the stock would be inflated on the strength of their promise to overhaul the collections and create a completely new organization. Once the stock was sold, however, they would pocket the profits, resign from the museum company, and leave the stockholders holding the bag.

Between his work at the Bowery Amphitheatre and his articles in the Sunday papers, Barnum had plenty of friends in the newspaper business. He persuaded them to publish a series of articles warning the public against buying the stock. The stories ridiculed the idea of merging the two museums and pointed out that the directors were primarily bankers who didn't know the first thing about running a museum.

The newspaper campaign forced the directors to postpone their plans to sell stock and wait until the furor died down. In the meantime, they decided to buy Barnum's silence by offering him a job as manager of the combined museums. Barnum accepted but demanded an outrageously high salary. The directors were so eager to shut him up that they readily agreed.

Without their knowledge, however, he extracted a promise from John Heath that if the New York Museum Company directors did not make their final payment as promised on December 26, his $12,000 offer would be accepted.

Having bought off their sole rival with the promise of a good job, the New York Museum directors saw no need to rush. December 26 came and went and their final payment remained due. This time, John Heath kept his word. By the following afternoon, the necessary papers had been signed and the American Museum was in the hands of Phineas Taylor Barnum.

The new owner took gleeful revenge on his rivals and would-be employers by sending them a note offering them free admission to the American Museum whenever they wished. It was signed "P. T. Barnum, Proprietor."

Barnum's Museum

Barnum's American Museum opened on New Year's Day 1842. Anyone who passed the place could see at a glance that things had changed. Flags of every nation hung from the rooftop and balconies, and multicolored banners announced the various exhibits. By night the building was bathed in limelight that emanated from a pair of giant searchlights trained on its facade.

Unable to afford any new exhibits until he paid off his debt to Francis Olmsted, Barnum had to make the most of what he had. He deluged the public with ads that described even the most ordinary items as amazing, astounding, unique, or incredible. He also developed various gimmicks that called attention to the museum.

For a long while, he paid a band to play on the front balcony. Their performances were billed as free outdoor concerts, and crowds of people showed up to hear them. But he always hired the worst band he could find, and the concertgoers invariably fled into the museum to escape from the din.

On one occasion, a man showed up at the box office begging for money. Instead of giving him a handout, Barnum put him to work. He gave the man five bricks and told him to place each one at a given point starting at the corner of Broadway and Ann Street.

After he had disposed of the first four bricks, the man was to use the fifth one to replace the first and so on down the line. If anyone asked what he was doing, the man was to keep mum, but at the end of every hour, he was to march into the American Museum, walk through all the exhibition halls, then march out and resume his work.

The man did as he was told, and within thirty minutes a huge crowd had gathered along Broadway trying to figure out what he was up to. Within the hour the crowd had doubled, and each time the man entered the museum, at least a dozen rubberneckers bought tickets and marched in after him.

The bricklaying routine continued for several days and was halted only after the police complained about the crowds obstructing the sidewalk. By then the stunt had accomplished its purpose. There was a sharp increase in ticket sales, and many New Yorkers who had not visited the place in years decided it was time they went back.

The first American Museum as it appeared circa 1850. Under Barnum's management, the museum outgrew the five-story building and expanded into the upper floors of several adjacent structures. *(Courtesy of Barnum Museum, Bridgeport, Connecticut)*

In less than two years, the American Museum was doing so well that Barnum was able to pay off his debt to Francis Olmsted and become its legal owner. His profits could now be spent on new exhibits and bigger and better promotional schemes.

Jugglers, glassblowers, ventriloquists, and magicians were booked into the Lecture Room. Another attraction was a giant, Robert Hales, who was seven and a half feet tall and weighed over 450 pounds, and a giantess, Eliza Simpson, who was almost as large. When the pair fell in love, Barnum arranged for them to get married at the museum before a paying audience.

Easterners were fascinated by Indians, so Barnum recruited a band of them in Iowa and paid them to entertain his customers by performing some of their tribal dances. They settled in on the fifth floor of the museum, cooking their meals in the fireplace and sleeping on the floor.

Special shows and contests were another big draw. In addition to flower shows, dog shows, and bird shows, the American Museum sponsored baby shows with a $100 prize awarded to the handsomest, the fattest, or the brightest child, and beauty contests in which the public was invited to submit daguerreotypes to find "the handsomest woman in America."

In his quest for unique promotional stunts, Barnum commissioned a set of enormous paintings of wild animals and had them installed between the upper-story windows in the middle of the night. The sight stopped traffic on Broadway the next morning and enticed still more people to come in and see their real-life counterparts in the museum's zoo.

Within a few years, Barnum's American Museum was one of New York's favorite entertainment spots. On holidays, the crowds were often so large that prospective ticket buyers had to be turned away. The main reason, Barnum discovered, was that many of his customers were stretching their visits into all-day outings. They would bring the children and pack a lunch. Then, instead of leaving after they had seen the exhibits, they would go back and tour the whole museum for a second, and sometimes a third, time.

Barnum was concerned about how much this was costing him in lost ticket sales, but he didn't know what to do about it until one day he came across one of his scene painters at work.

"Here," he said to the man, "take a piece of canvas four feet square and paint on it in large letters: TO THE EGRESS."

When the sign was finished, Barnum directed the man to nail it over the door to the back stairs that led out to Ann Street. The crowds, unaware that "egress" was simply another word for exit, thought they were being directed toward a new exhibit.

"The aigress," Barnum heard an Irish woman remark. "Sure, that's an animal we haven't seen."

Following the sign, the crowds descended the staircase and found themselves out in the street. Meanwhile,

44

the museum's box office was briskly selling tickets to the new customers lined up along Broadway waiting to take their places.

In his efforts to maintain a constant flow of new attractions, Barnum regularly traded exhibits and performers with a Boston museum owner named Moses Kimball. Sometimes the two men would chip in to buy an exhibit and take turns displaying it at their establishments.

Barnum once offered Kimball "a pretty good sized bald eagle skin." On another occasion he appealed to him for help in finding fresh exhibits: "I *must* have a fat boy or other monster, something new *in the course of this week.*"

No matter what the attraction, however, the price had to be right. Barnum was very firm about that; he hated to lose money on any deal. He complained only half jokingly when one of his best finds, an orangutan, developed a fatal illness after he had already invested in a large flag, posters, and newspaper engravings to advertise its arrival.

One joint venture that earned Barnum a great deal of money also caused him a great deal of grief. It was a curiosity called the Fejee Mermaid, which Moses Kimball had purchased from a man whose father, a sea captain, had bought from some Japanese sailors.

The so-called mermaid was an ugly dried-up object about three feet long, with the body of a fish and the head and hands of a monkey. The two parts had been

The Fejee Mermaid. The bogus mermaid is still in existence. After Moses Kimball's death, it was acquired along with hundreds of other objects from his museum by the Peabody Museum at Harvard University. (*Courtesy of Peabody Museum, Harvard University*)

joined together so cleverly that it was impossible to see where they met. Thus, anyone who was gullible enough to believe in mermaids in the first place could easily conclude that the Fejee Mermaid was the real thing.

Before installing the curiosity in the American Museum, Barnum created some advance publicity by sending it on tour and trying to give it a dimension of credibility. The New York press began picking up stories from out-of-town newspapers about a British naturalist, Dr. Griffin, who was passing through the United States on his way back to England after a world tour. In the course of his travels, the reports said, Dr. Griffin had accumulated several exotic objects, including a mermaid that had been captured in the Fejee Islands.

In reality, Dr. Griffin was Levi Lyman, the same man who had put Joice Heth through her paces. No one recognized him in his new role, and the advance reports of his arrival in New York made everyone eager to see his amazing acquisition. The Fejee Mermaid was exhibited at a hall on Broadway where Dr. Griffin delivered a solemn lecture on natural science and proposed several erudite theories that might explain the strange phenomenon.

After a one-week appearance at the hall, and several front-page newspaper reports of the event, the Fejee Mermaid moved on to the American Museum. By then, thousands of New Yorkers were clamoring to see it. Even people who scoffed at the idea of mermaids couldn't resist taking a look.

When ticket sales slowed down in New York, Barnum packed up the Fejee Mermaid for another tour. This time his uncle, Alanson Taylor, was her escort. The tour was a success until they reached Charleston, South Carolina. There, John Bachman, a local naturalist and Lutheran minister, attacked the exhibit as a fraud, pointing out what should have been obvious all along: The mermaid was actually the head and hands of a monkey sewn to the body of a fish.

Bachman stirred up so much hostility that Alanson Taylor quietly shipped the mermaid back to New York and left Charleston as quickly as possible. Instead of being embarrassed by Bachman's attack, Barnum was inclined to brazen it out. He tried to persuade Moses Kimball, who owned the mermaid, to bring a lawsuit against Bachman. Kimball refused, so he let the matter drop, but if it had been Barnum's choice, he almost certainly would have gone ahead. Even if he lost, the publicity would have kept the Fejee Mermaid in the public eye and made it a more profitable exhibit than ever.

After the Fejee Mermaid episode, Barnum was again denounced as a humbug, just as he had been when the truth about Joice Heth came out. But he never apologized for the deception. Quite the opposite.

In the first edition of his autobiography, which was published in 1855, he discussed the Fejee Mermaid at some length. Then, in a bid to promote the book, he retrieved the object from Moses Kimball and installed it in the American Museum for a second time. He urged the public to come see the curiosity that had stirred up so much controversy. With typical Barnum humor, the exhibit opened on April Fools' Day.

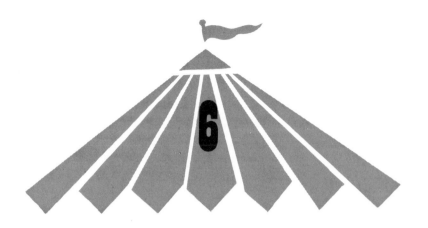

General Tom Thumb

Less than a year after the Fejee Mermaid was smuggled out of Charleston, P. T. Barnum came across a new and far more extraordinary exhibit. This one had the added advantage of being absolutely authentic.

Barnum's half brother Philo, who ran a hotel in Bridgeport, Connecticut, told him about a remarkably small boy who lived nearby. The next time Barnum was in Bridgeport, he asked to meet the child and was soon introduced to Charles Sherwood Stratton. The boy was a healthy, bright-eyed, perfectly normal five-year-old, except for the fact that he was less than two feet tall and weighed a mere fifteen pounds.

Charley Stratton's incredibly small size was caused by a defective pituitary gland, the part of the brain that controls growth. There wasn't much that could be done

Barnum and Tom Thumb. Under Barnum's management, the poor, uneducated boy grew into a rich and sophisticated man with a stable of fine horses and a custom-designed yacht. (*Courtesy of Barnum Museum, Bridgeport, Connecticut*)

about his condition, but even if medical help had been available, the Strattons were too poor to afford it.

Although Charley was something of a curiosity around Bridgeport, he managed to lead a reasonably normal life—at least until P. T. Barnum came along. One look at Charley Stratton and Barnum knew he had found the exhibit that could make his fortune. He had a long talk with the boy's parents, and by the time it was over, they had agreed to let Charley go to New York with his mother and appear for four weeks at the American Museum.

The instant he returned to New York, Barnum set about publicizing the event. First, he rewrote Charley Stratton's biography. He raised his age from five to eleven to make his diminutive size seem even more incredible. Then he gave him a new name and a military rank, General Tom Thumb. Knowing that American audiences were always more impressed with entertainment from abroad, Barnum also billed him as "just arrived from England."

The General was an appealing fellow. He had fair hair, bright eyes, and a cheerful smile. To get some advance publicity for his appearance at the museum, Barnum took him to visit some of the city's newspaper editors. Tom succeeded in charming them by climbing onto their desks and hopping around among their inkpots and papers.

Barnum's "man in miniature," as he liked to call him, turned out to be more than an attractive curiosity.

He was good at memorizing lines and was very much at ease on the stage. Barnum taught him several song-and-dance numbers, along with a poem about being small. As part of his act, Tom also donned various costumes—Napoleon, Cupid, a Revolutionary War soldier—and made amusing comments about each of his roles.

In addition to all his other talents, General Tom Thumb was amazingly quick-witted. If something unexpected happened in the course of an appearance, he could always ad lib a clever remark or concoct some piece of stage business to rescue the situation. When the General's four-week engagement was over, Barnum signed him up for a full year at double his original salary.

New Year's Day 1844 marked the second anniversary of P. T. Barnum's ownership of the American Museum. It was doing so well that he had no qualms about leaving it in the hands of his manager while he took on the challenge of making General Tom Thumb the toast of Europe.

On January 18, Barnum sailed for England with the boy and his parents, Sherwood and Cynthia Stratton, and H. G. Sherman, another showman whom he had hired as Tom Thumb's tutor. Charity Barnum stayed home. She was nervous about ocean voyages and she also had a new baby daughter, Frances, to care for.

Barnum's plan for introducing Tom Thumb to the British public was nothing if not ambitious. He aimed to start at the very top. If he could wangle an audience for

Tom with Queen Victoria and the Queen found him amusing—which Barnum was sure she would—he would vault to instant celebrity and the money would come rolling in.

When their ship docked at Liverpool, however, Barnum discovered that his plan was in trouble. The Queen's father-in-law had just died. The Royal Family was in mourning and there would be no audiences until further notice. Trying to make the best of the situation, Barnum booked Tom into a Liverpool theater, billing him as "the Greatest Natural Curiosity in the World . . . the SMALLEST PERSON that ever WALKED ALONE!"

The Liverpudlians could not have cared less. They were not especially interested in dwarfs, and they certainly weren't going to pay a shilling—the equivalent of about twenty-five cents—to see one.

Barnum and his party moved on to London, where he booked the General into the Princess Theater for a three-day engagement. Again he got a tepid reception, so Barnum took a different tack. There were no more public appearances. Instead, the showman rented a mansion in a fashionable section of town and engaged a staff of servants. As soon as he had settled in, he invited all the lords and ladies, dukes and duchesses, and barons and earls in London to a private meeting with General Tom Thumb.

Tom's performances were the highlight of these evenings, and as the word of his talent spread, he found himself being summoned to appear in some of London's most elegant drawing rooms. When it was time to go home, a purse full of gold coins was discreetly pressed into Barnum's hand.

Still hoping for an invitation to Buckingham Palace, Barnum asked Edward Everett, the United States Minister to the Court of St. James, to put in a good word for his fellow Americans. Everett went even further. He arranged for them to meet the Master of the Royal Household, Charles Augustus Murray.

Unlike most British aristocrats, Murray did not look down his nose at Americans. He had traveled widely in the United States and published a favorable account of his experiences. Murray was not only charmed by Tom Thumb, he thought the Royal Family was ready for a little cheering up after their weeks of mourning. Before long, one of the Queen's Life Guards, in full uniform, arrived at the door of Barnum's rented mansion with the coveted invitation for General Tom Thumb and his guardian, Mr. Barnum.

The visiting Americans spent over an hour with the Queen and her other guests. Tom performed a few of his songs and dances, then he and the Queen had a private chat. Victoria was twenty-five years old at the time and was not the dour figure she became in her later years. She enjoyed Tom's quick wit and was delighted when he provided the company with a final bit of humor as he was leaving.

Following the court custom, Barnum and the General backed away from the Queen so they would continue facing her as they left the room. But Tom's legs were so much shorter than Barnum's that he quickly fell behind. Every once in a while he would turn around, scamper a few feet until he caught up, and then resume his backward progress.

The Queen's guests were greatly amused at the sight. There was even more laughter when, as the two Americans were making their exit, the Queen's pet poodle suddenly charged at Tom and began barking ferociously. To everyone's delight, the boy brandished the tiny cane he carried and started fencing with the dog.

In the course of his audience, Tom Thumb had inquired after the Queen's son, Edward, Prince of Wales. The Prince had already been put to bed, but Tom was invited to come back for a visit with him and his older sister, Princess Victoria. Edward, who was barely three years old, was already several inches taller than his American visitor.

"The Prince is taller than I am," Tom remarked amiably, "but I *feel* as big as anybody." With that, he strutted up and down the room with a jaunty smile that made everyone laugh.

Ever since his arrival in England, Barnum had been trying to get some newspaper coverage for the General. So far he had not had any luck, but he was hoping that their audience with Queen Victoria would turn the tide. Every paper in London published the Court Circular, which listed all the distinguished visitors to Buckingham Palace.

The editor of the Circular happened to be at the palace on the day Tom Thumb was presented. Barnum drew him aside and expressed the hope that Tom's audience would be included in his report. The editor, who was used to listing ambassadors and heads of state, was not sure what to say about a dwarf, so he asked Barnum to do the honors.

A day or two later, every newspaper in London carried a report that established Tom Thumb as England's newest celebrity: "The American Dwarf, General Tom Thumb, accompanied by his guardian, Mr. P. T. Barnum of New York, had the honour of attending the Palace on Saturday evening, when the General exhibited his clever imitations of Napoleon, etc., which elicited the approbation of Her Majesty and the Royal Circle."

Once Tom Thumb received the royal stamp of approval, everyone in London felt obligated to see him. Barnum leased a large hall, and the rest was easy. On some days, as many as fifty or sixty carriages waited outside the hall while their owners enjoyed the show.

The General's popularity was so extensive that his portrait hung in shop windows and his likeness was reproduced on plates, mugs, and fans. Tom Thumb dolls were sold in the shops, songs were written in his honor, and there was even a children's dance called the General Tom Thumb Polka.

The General made many more visits to Buckingham

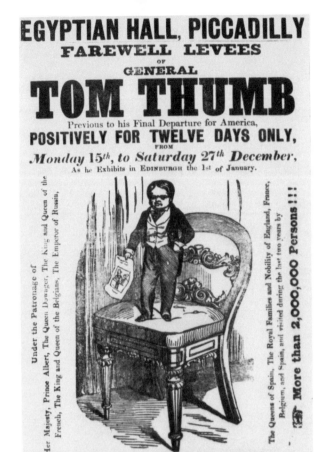

A poster advertising Tom Thumb's farewell appearance in London. His farewell tour of England lasted a full year with no less than three "final" engagements at Egyptian Hall. (*Courtesy of Barnum Museum, Bridgeport, Connecticut*)

Palace. He became such a favorite that Barnum hired a tailor to make him a special court costume. It consisted of a brown velvet coat and breeches, with an embroidered vest, white silk stockings and pumps, and a cocked hat and dress sword.

To complete the picture, a carriage maker was commissioned to build a custom-made carriage for Tom to ride in. Eleven inches wide and twenty inches high, it was painted white and blue and drawn by four miniature Shetland ponies, each only twenty-eight inches tall.

The carriage cost over $2,000—more than most people earned in a year—but Barnum could easily afford it. Tom Thumb's visits to Buckingham Palace had been rewarded with expensive gifts and gold coins. His public performances brought in hundreds of dollars a day, and Barnum was also collecting the proceeds from the Tom Thumb booklets and souvenirs that sold by the thousands.

After his success in England, the General toured Europe and was received at most of the royal courts. In Paris, he was invited to ride in his private carriage in the fashionable Longchamp procession, an annual parade celebrating the arrival of Easter. He was also showered with gifts. France's King Louis Philippe gave him an emerald-and-diamond brooch and Queen Isabella II of Spain presented him with a solid-gold chain. On a return visit to Buckingham Palace, the Dowager Queen Adelaide, widow of Queen Victoria's uncle and predecessor, King William IV, gave him a miniature gold watch.

Having successfully launched General Tom Thumb, P. T. Barnum left him under the management of his tutor, H. G. Sherman, and went off to tour Europe on his own. Before leaving the United States, he had signed on as a roving correspondent for the New York *Atlas*. He had already sent the newspaper several letters about his travels, but with Tom Thumb in someone else's charge, he would have more time not only to write but to look for new attractions for his museum.

The two occupations were a neat fit. When he came across a company of Swiss Bell Ringers, who were actually English, he wrote a glowing account of their performance, remarking that some smart showman ought to sign them up for a tour of the United States. What he didn't mention was that he had already signed them up himself.

In the course of his travels, he acquired several new items for his museum, including a set of Queen Victoria's royal robes and an exhibition of animals that were natural enemies—cats and dogs, owls and mice, hawks and sparrows—but lived together in harmony in the same cage. Barnum christened the exhibit The Happy Family, and it became one of the American Museum's most popular attractions.

After a visit to Shakespeare's birthplace at Stratford-on-Avon, he conceived the idea of buying the house and having it dismantled and transported to New York. He was already negotiating the deal when the news leaked out. Horrified at the thought of a national treasure being shipped out of the country, a group of Britons promptly formed the Shakespeare Association and purchased the building on its behalf.

There was one sad note in Barnum's trip. While he was away, his daughter Frances died a few weeks short of her second birthday. It took four weeks for the news to reach him, and his sorrow was accentuated by the fact that he had just shipped her a box of toys.

Barnum returned to New York in the fall of 1844 to renew his lease on the property on which the American Museum stood. He did not notify Charity of the date of his arrival, and when his ship docked, he went straight to the museum. There he sent her an unsigned message telling her to come at once to the museum to meet with a gentleman who had just arrived from Europe and carried a message meant for her ears only.

Needless to say, Charity was astonished and delighted to be reunited with her husband. When he returned to England three weeks later, she and Caroline and Helen went with him. They rented a house in London and enjoyed a lively social life. Wherever he went, Barnum always collected plenty of friends. Even people who were disposed to dislike him were usually won over by his genial manner and his talent for telling a good story.

Charity and the girls returned to New York that summer, and the following spring, Charity gave birth to another daughter, Pauline, who would become her father's favorite. Barnum came home to see his new little daughter and spend three months with his family. Then it was back to Europe for another round of touring with Tom Thumb and another search for new exhibits.

By the time P. T. Barnum and his entourage returned to the United States at the beginning of 1847, they had been traveling for almost three years. The General had been such a hit in every country he visited that Barnum could honestly bill him as an international sensation.

After a four-week engagement at the American Museum, where he played to consistently full houses, Tom Thumb again went on tour. He visited Cuba and Canada, along with every important city in the United States. In Washington, D.C., he was invited to the White House to give a special performance for President and Mrs. James Polk.

Although Barnum no longer toured with Tom Thumb, under the terms of his contract with the Strattons he continued to receive a generous percentage of his income. Between the money he made from his man in miniature and the awesome success of the American Museum, Phineas Taylor Barnum had become a very rich man.

The Swedish Nightingale

During the three months he spent in the United States when he came home to see his baby daughter, P. T. Barnum bought seventeen acres of land fronting on Long Island Sound in Fairfield, Connecticut. He knew the area from visiting his half brother in Bridgeport, and he thought it would be a fine place to build a house.

In his travels through England, Barnum had visited the seaside resort of Brighton and was quite taken with the Oriental domes and delicate carvings on the Royal Pavilion, the summer palace built by one of Queen Victoria's predecessors, King George IV. Barnum commissioned an architect to design a replica of the ornate structure and hired a contractor to build it, while he returned to Europe to complete his tour with General Tom Thumb.

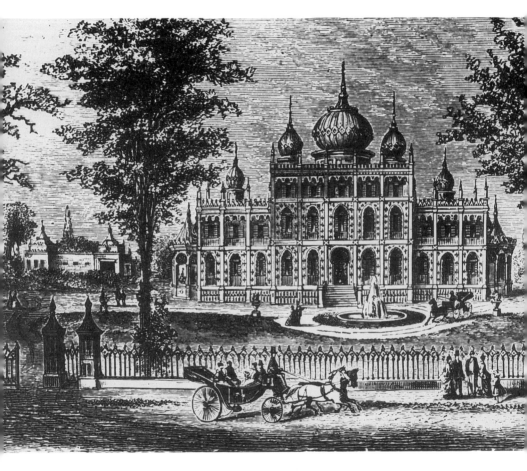

Iranistan. Like almost everything Barnum did, the mansion was designed to attract attention. Although the house was destroyed by fire, the name is commemorated in Bridgeport's Iranistan Avenue. (*Courtesy of Barnum Museum, Bridgeport, Connecticut*)

The mansion, which was finished in the fall of 1848, bore no resemblance to any other building in the country. The great P. T., as the public had taken to calling him, had built himself a sultan's palace. Executed in rust-colored sandstone, it was capped with domes and spires and adorned with intricately carved arches that framed the broad piazzas on each of its three floors. Barnum called it Iranistan, which means "Oriental Villa."

The inside of the mansion was equally striking. In the spacious center hallway, a carved walnut staircase spiraled upward to the most dramatic room in the house—the large central dome at the very top. This lofty sitting room boasted a circular divan that could accommodate forty-five people. It had diamond-shaped windows set with panes of different-colored glass. The various colors cast an unusual glow on the landscape and turned the outside world into a fairyland.

Barnum spared no expense on the mansion. It had marble fireplaces, gilt ceilings, elaborately carved doors, and a dining room that could seat forty people. But he struck a bargain on some of the furnishings. While he was in Paris, the estate of a Russian prince was auctioned off. There were many valuable items, including a set of silver flatware, a gold tea set, and some rare china. They could have commanded staggering prices, but their value had been diminished by the fact that they bore the prince's monogram and coat of arms.

That didn't bother Barnum. He snapped up the entire lot. The prince's initials were P. T., so he had an engraver add a final *B*. As for the coat of arms, it could well have been created with Barnum in mind. The motto on the escutcheon was "Love God and Be Merry."

As the American Museum continued to thrive, Barnum used a share of his profits to buy another museum in Philadelphia, which he called, "P. T. Barnum's Museum of Living Wonders." He moved his exhibits back and forth between the two establishments, as he had once done with his friend Moses Kimball in Boston.

A visitor to one or the other of the museums might see the black pianist Old Blind Tom, who could play any piece of music after hearing it only once; Young Herman the Expansionist, who with one deep breath could increase his chest measurement from thirty-eight to sixty inches; or Madame Josephine Fortune Clofullia, who sported a full-grown beard. At both museums, the menagerie was still a major attraction, and in New York, there was an aquarium as well. Stocked with a large collection of native and exotic fishes, including sharks, it was the first public aquarium in the country.

The entertainment in the Lecture Room included a full program of concerts, dramatic readings, and plays. Among the latter was a melodrama called *The Drunkard*, which portrayed the evils of alcohol. The play ran for a solid one hundred and fifty performances. Its choice was no accident: Barnum belonged to the Temperance Movement, which aimed to abolish the manufacture and sale of alcoholic beverages.

As a younger man, he had never hesitated to take a

drink, and during his travels through Europe, he had downed his share of fine wines and brandies. In the course of a visit to Saratoga to exhibit Tom Thumb at the New York State Agricultural Fair, however, he saw so much drunkenness and disorderly behavior that he turned against alcohol. He not only stopped drinking himself, he took to the lecture platform to persuade others to follow his example.

After being so violently attacked for trying to pass off the Fejee Mermaid as a genuine mermaid, Barnum tried to steer clear of phony exhibits. But when a good opportunity presented itself, the showman couldn't resist. During a visit to Cincinnati, someone offered him an odd-looking horse. It had no mane or tail, and its hide was covered with a coat of thick curly hair that looked exactly like wool. Barnum paid $500 for the creature. Although he had no plans for it at the time, he knew he'd think of something.

Of course, he did. Not long after Barnum acquired the "Woolly Horse," the Western explorer Colonel John C. Fremont survived a daring midwinter expedition through the Rocky Mountains to California. Fremont's adventures were the talk of the country, and P. T. Barnum's fertile imagination instantly clicked into gear.

The Woolly Horse was put on display. It was actually just a freak of nature, but with Barnum in charge it became a rare form of wildlife "made up of the Elephant, Deer, Horse, Buffalo, Camel and Sheep." He compounded the tale by claiming that it had been captured by Colonel Fremont in the course of his expedition through the Rockies.

Despite its unusual history, the Woolly Horse attracted only moderate interest in New York and Philadelphia. When Barnum sent it on tour to Washington, D.C., however, his profits soared. Fremont's father-in-law, Senator Thomas Hart Benton, took great exception to the exhibit and declared the Woolly Horse a fake. He had received dozens of letters from his son-in-law after he completed his expedition, he said, and not one of them contained any mention of finding such an animal.

The Senator was so infuriated that he sued Barnum's agent for taking money from him—his twenty-five-cent admission charge—under false pretenses. Benton lost, but the newspaper reports of the charges gave the Woolly Horse pages of free publicity and made it the most profitable exhibit in Washington.

In spite of the pleasure he took in collecting freaks and curiosities to exhibit at his museums, P. T. Barnum had long harbored a secret wish to have his name associated with more distinguished types of entertainment. It was this wish that inspired him to introduce the singer Jenny Lind to American audiences.

The Swedish Nightingale, as she was called, had been hailed in Europe as the greatest soprano of the age. When she gave a concert in London, Queen Victoria was so entranced that she tossed her own bouquet of flowers at her feet.

Jenny Lind's life story was almost as remarkable as

A portrait of Jenny Lind. The "Swedish Nightingale" looked and sang like an angel, but offstage she could be moody, demanding, and rude. *(Courtesy of Barnum Museum, Bridgeport, Connecticut)*

her voice. As a poor and lonely little girl in Stockholm, she often sang in the street. One day she was overheard by a famous dancer who arranged for her to audition at Stockholm's Royal Theater. The theater director was not particularly interested in listening to a nine-year-old, but when he heard her sing, he immediately offered to provide her with voice lessons free of charge.

From this fairy-tale beginning, Jenny Lind had gone on to become a famous opera star. By the time Barnum became interested in her, however, she had given up opera for the concert stage. She still performed some of her favorite arias, but having become deeply religious, she preferred to sing sacred music such as Handel's *Messiah*. She also favored the simple folk songs of her native Scandinavia, which she sang with such beauty and feeling that invariably her audiences were moved to tears.

Although Jenny Lind was amply rewarded for her talent, she kept only a modest share of the lavish sums she earned. Most of it went to support hospitals and orphan asylums and to provide musical training for poor but gifted young people.

When Barnum contacted Jenny Lind's agents about the possibility of an American tour, they didn't object to the plan but they drove a hard bargain. Under the terms of the contract Barnum signed with them, the soprano would spend a year and a half touring the United States giving a total of one hundred and fifty concerts. She would receive a fee of $150,000—payable in advance. In addition, Barnum would be responsible for the salaries of two servants, her musical director, and a male singer to accompany her in duets. He was also expected to pay the travel and hotel expenses for the entire party.

These sums did not include the costs of booking concert halls, hiring an orchestra, printing tickets, and taking out ads for her concerts. The total was daunting even for a rich man like P. T. Barnum. Nevertheless, the showman was determined to go ahead. He sold several pieces of real estate he had invested in, mortgaged several others, and borrowed the last $5,000 he needed from an old friend.

Barnum was taking a huge gamble in bringing Jenny Lind to America. She was a serious concert singer, not a music hall star. There was no evidence that she would appeal to the general public, and if she didn't, Barnum was going to lose a small fortune. With that much money at stake, not to mention his reputation as an unerring judge of public taste, P. T. Barnum mounted the most extensive advertising and publicity campaign of his career.

The showman's contract with Jenny Lind was signed in January 1850, but she did not arrive in New York until September 1. Barnum took advantage of the delay to whet the public's appetite. He planted stories about the singer's beauty and her goodness in the New York dailies and played up the fact that she regarded her voice as a gift from God. It was an era of strong adherence to religion and morality, and Barnum was well

WELCOME TO JENNY LIND.

Jenny Lind's arrival in America. The triumphal arches were erected at Barnum's request and the crowd was swelled by the presence of several dozen employees of the American Museum. (*Courtesy of Barnum Museum, Bridgeport, Connecticut*)

aware that the American public would be more favorably disposed to a singer with an unblemished private life.

Barnum also played up the unique beauty of Jenny Lind's singing voice. When she gave a farewell concert in Liverpool shortly before sailing for America, he arranged to have a glowing review reprinted in several New York papers.

By the time Jenny Lind's ship arrived in New York, the showman had stirred up so much interest that a crowd of several thousand people was on hand to greet her. More crowds lined the streets as she rode to her hotel, and another mob gathered outside and cheered loudly when Barnum led her out on the balcony of her suite for her first public appearance.

Jenny Lind was to make her American debut at Castle Garden at the tip of Manhattan Island. Originally built as a fort, the building had been converted into a large auditorium that was the scene of some of New York's most notable public events. Barnum hoped to fill the house, but he was taking no chances. To convince New Yorkers that hearing Jenny Lind would be a once-in-a-lifetime experience, he announced an auction at which the first ticket would be sold to the highest bidder.

The auction was designed to get added press coverage for the concert and to incite a stampede to the box office. Barnum advised several of his friends not to be too cautious in their bidding, because the publicity would be as good for their own businesses as it was for his. He was right.

John Genin, who owned a hat shop next door to the American Museum, outbid his closest rival and bought the first ticket for $225. It was an outrageous sum, since the best seats in the house cost only a fraction of that amount, but the bid made Genin famous. New Yorkers and tourists alike rushed to buy Genin hats, and he quickly became the most successful hatter in the country.

The Swedish Nightingale made her American debut on the evening of September 11, 1850. Some six thousand people filled Castle Garden for the concert. To facilitate the seating and create yet another news story, Barnum had the auditorium divided into four sections and assigned each a different color. The sections were marked off by lamps of the appropriate color, the tickets for each section were printed in the same color, and the ushers wore rosettes to match.

Jenny Lind did not disappoint her audience. She was every bit as lovely as they had been led to believe, and her voice was equally enchanting. The crowds clapped, cheered, and shouted their enthusiasm, and the applause was even louder when Barnum stepped on stage to announce that Miss Lind would donate ten thousand dollars from her share of the concert's profits to several of New York's most worthy charities.

As a result of the hoopla created by Barnum, the city—indeed the entire country—was seized with

"Lindomania." A British magazine ran an article describing the singer as "Jenny the First—Queen of the Americans." They weren't far wrong. The Swedish Nightingale was greeted by cheering crowds wherever she went. People clamored for her autograph. One man retrieved a glove she had dropped and charged people for the privilege of kissing it.

In addition, the singer's picture appeared on dishes, fans, flasks, and trivets. Jenny Lind figurines were prized knickknacks, and Jenny Lind bonnets became the latest style.

Jenny Lind's American tour included appearances in over a dozen major cities, with a side trip to Havana, Cuba. Ticket auctions like the one held in New York became the accepted method of promoting her concerts. In Boston, the high bid was $625; in Providence, $650. Jenny also followed the custom she had established in New York of donating her share of the opening-night profits to local charities.

Despite—or more likely, because of—the Swedish Nightingale's immense popularity, many people resented the fact that such a gifted singer had gotten involved with such a fast-talking promoter as P. T. Barnum. There were rumors that he was cheating her out of her fees, browbeating hotel owners to give her free lodgings, and making her concerts such must-see events that people of modest means were going into debt to buy tickets.

To further discredit Barnum, his critics dredged up

his old tricks—Joice Heth, the Fejee Mermaid, Fremont's Woolly Horse—and accused him once again of being a humbug. A few went so far as to suggest that Jenny was in on the plot and that beneath her sweet, demure manner, she was every bit as mercenary as her manager. One wit wrote a poem to that effect:

> They'll welcome you with speeches and serenades
>   and rockets
> And you will touch their hearts and I will touch
>   their pockets
> And if between us both the public isn't skinned
> Why my name isn't Barnum, nor your name Jenny
>   Lind.

The attacks had no effect. The public refused to break off their love affair with Jenny Lind. They loved her singing. They loved her innocence and generosity. And they loved P. T. Barnum for giving them the opportunity to see her.

But the partnership between P. T. Barnum and Jenny Lind soon faltered. In June 1851, after giving ninety-six concerts in slightly less than ten months, Jenny Lind decided to break her contract with the showman. Someone—possibly her pianist, Otto Goldschmidt, whom she had married in the course of her tour—had persuaded her that she no longer needed Barnum as her manager.

Although Jenny Lind stayed in America for another

eleven months, her popularity sank dramatically. The excitement created by her arrival may simply have been too intense to sustain, but there is another equally valid explanation: With no more P. T. Barnum to ballyhoo her talents, she stopped being one of the wonders of the world and became just another soprano.

In spite of their severed relationship, Barnum and Jenny remained on friendly terms. She always sent him complimentary tickets when she gave concerts in New York, and he went backstage to say good-bye when she made her final appearance at Castle Garden before returning to Europe with her husband.

If Barnum had any hard feelings about being deserted by Jenny Lind, he never gave any sign of it. He certainly had no reason to regret having brought her to America. The concert tour she made under his management grossed over $700,000. Even when the singer's share and the expenses of the tour were paid, it was still a tidy sum. In addition, the adulation and attention that Jenny Lind received reflected favorably on Barnum and helped to promote his museums.

P. T. Barnum was pleased that his biggest gamble had paid off so handsomely, but he also took great pride in having introduced Jenny Lind to American audiences. He felt that he had made a significant contribution to culture by persuading ordinary people to appreciate and enjoy a classical singer. When the showman looked back over his achievements in later years, Jenny Lind's concert tour was the one of which he was most proud.

Barnum Goes Bust

Shortly before P. T. Barnum and Jenny Lind agreed to go their separate ways, the showman put together "Barnum's Great Asiatic Caravan, Museum and Menagerie"—a traveling version of the American Museum, with General Tom Thumb as its star. He launched it with a mammoth parade up Broadway. Among its wonders was a herd of ten elephants harnessed in pairs and pulling a chariot.

When he sold the enterprise four years later, Barnum kept one of the elephants and had it shipped to Connecticut. A portion of the property on which his Oriental villa stood had been turned into a working farm, and six acres of cultivated land lay along the tracks of the New York and New Haven Railroad.

Barnum hitched the elephant to a plow, dressed its

78

The elephant as farm animal. The pachyderm plowed the same six acres more than sixty times before Barnum abandoned the publicity stunt and sold the animal to a privately owned zoo. (*Courtesy of Barnum Museum, Bridgeport, Connecticut*)

keeper in an Oriental costume, and handed him a time-table. Then he ordered him to lead the elephant to the field along the railroad tracks and to start plowing every time a train was scheduled to pass by.

The sight of the elephant plowing the field never failed to astonish the railroad passengers, and news of the marvel spread quickly. Newspapers all over the world published pictures of the elephant. Whenever they wrote him up, P. T. Barnum and the American Museum got mentioned too.

Several papers reported that in addition to doing farm work, the pachyderm also watered the lawn, planted corn, picked fruit, and even fetched the mail from the post office with his trunk. As a result, every farmer in the country began to believe that P. T. Barnum had discovered a phenomenal new work animal. The leaders of several state and county agricultural societies wrote to request further information.

Barnum wrote back and assured them that as a work animal, the elephant was no match for the horse, the mule, or the ox. It did have another important value, however: It was an excellent advertisement for his museum.

Always on the lookout for new outlets for his energies, Barnum explored a number of sidelines to the museum business. At one point, he invested in a company that sold fire extinguishers. At another, he started a weekly newspaper. Neither went well. He had no better luck when he took over the management of the Crystal Palace. The huge glass-and-iron building had been the site of the 1853 World's Fair, and its stockholders were hoping to run it as a permanent exhibition hall after the fair ended.

So far they had not been able to entice the public to make the trip uptown—the building was on Forty-second Street just west of Fifth Avenue. Even the great P. T. could not induce them to go so far out of their way, and he soon gave up. In 1856, the Crystal Palace was destroyed by fire.

Barnum must have been disappointed by the failure of these enterprises, but he was not inclined to brood about misfortunes. Besides, he had another venture in the works. On top of everything else he was doing, the showman found time to produce an autobiography, *The Life of P. T. Barnum, Written by Himself.*

It was a highly entertaining book, written in a down-to-earth style and covering everything from his boyhood in Bethel to his success with Jenny Lind. Along the way, the author took advantage of every opportunity he could find to defend himself against the people who had denounced him as a humbug. He conceded that he may have stretched the truth now and then, but he had never actually cheated anyone and his patrons always got their money's worth.

Like so many other things Barnum did, his autobiography touched off a controversy. His enemies were offended by his self-congratulatory tone and by the fact that he so shamelessly acknowledged—indeed boasted about—playing tricks on the public. But scores of other critics praised the book, because, intertwined with the tales of his adventures in show business, Barnum offered practical lessons for succeeding in business and emphasized the importance of hard work, good morals, and temperance.

Published in December 1854, just in time for the Christmas shopping season, the book became an instant best-seller and was almost as popular in Europe as it was in the United States.

Meanwhile, Phineas Taylor Barnum found another wonder to promote—the city of Bridgeport, which was within a stone's throw of his Fairfield home. At the time, Bridgeport was one of the most attractive and prosperous cities in Connecticut.

In addition to having a fine harbor and excellent rail transportation, the city was within easy striking distance of both New York and New England. Hoping to capitalize on Bridgeport's assets, Barnum formed a partnership with attorney William Noble and secured title to a large chunk of land across the Pequonnock River from the city.

The partners hired a surveyor to lay out streets and began selling lots. Their plan was to create a brand-new city, East Bridgeport, that would have its own factories, homes, schools, churches, and parks. They hoped to make it a model community. Buyers had to agree to keep their property neat and clean, and the designs of all the houses and stores had to be approved by Barnum and Noble. To make the new city more appealing to prospective residents, the two men petitioned to have the tolls removed from the bridge over the Pequonnock River that connected the area to Bridgeport, and built a footbridge to make it easier for pedestrians to get back and forth.

As his planned community slowly took shape, Barnum began to spend more and more time in Connecticut. He had a capable manager at the American Museum, so he made only occasional trips to New York to be sure things were running smoothly. There were more than enough activities to keep him busy in Bridgeport. In 1851, he became the first president of the Pequonnock Bank, a post he held for the next four years. Not surprisingly, he even managed to liven up the staid world of banking. The Pequonnock's notes bore likenesses of him and Jenny Lind, with an engraving of Iranistan between them.

P. T. Barnum served as president of the Fairfield County Agricultural Association and was a regular at its annual fairs. He became one of the pillars of Bridgeport's Universalist Church, paying for various improvements, providing generous gifts of money and property, and sending flowers from his greenhouses to decorate the altar. He also played a major role in founding Mountain Grove Cemetery, where he and his family and several of his associates, including Tom Thumb, were eventually buried.

Over the years, Bridgeport's town burial ground

had become sadly neglected. It was overgrown with weeds, horses and pigs wandered through it by day, and vagrants and thieves hid there at night. Barnum led a campaign to have the cemetery closed down. The burial association that owned it was allowed to exchange the land for plots in the larger and more attractive Mountain Grove Cemetery, and over three thousand coffins were disinterred and reburied in the newer site.

P. T. Barnum was roundly criticized for his part in the transaction. Some of the older families in town resented having the graves of their ancestors disturbed. They were even more irate when, after the last corpse had been moved from the old burial ground, Barnum and a partner bought the twelve-acre site. The two men divided it into lots, laid out streets, and turned the former eyesore into an attractive neighborhood.

As part of his efforts to lure business to East Bridgeport, Barnum formed a partnership with a clock manufacturer, Theodore Terry, and persuaded him to build a factory there. A year or so later, he learned that the Jerome Clock Company in New Haven might be interested in moving to the new city and merging with the Terry and Barnum Company.

Barnum made an appointment to meet with the company's president, Chauncey Jerome. Jerome was definitely interested in the move, but as part of the deal, he wanted Barnum to sign a sheaf of bank notes pledging to pay up to $110,000 worth of the Jerome Clock Company's debts. The company was worth many times that amount. Chauncey Jerome had letters from several highly respected bankers attesting to that fact. But as he explained, they had just gone through an unusually slow season and Jerome needed the notes to pay a few outstanding bills.

P. T. Barnum had no reason to doubt Chauncey Jerome's word. He was a wealthy man and, from all reports, an honest one as well. As it turned out, however, Mr. Jerome was neither as rich nor as honest as Barnum had been led to believe. On the contrary, his clock company was on the verge of bankruptcy. The bankers who had attested to its financial soundness were lying too. They planned to use Barnum's notes to collect on their own loans to Jerome.

Unaware of all this, Barnum accepted Chauncey Jerome's proposition. He agreed to sign the bank notes. Then Barnum, a normally astute businessman, made a foolish mistake. He didn't keep track of the notes he was signing. A few months later, he discovered that the clock manufacturer had taken advantage of his trust and bilked him out of a cool $500,000.

Fortunately, Barnum was able to stave off the worst of the disaster. As soon as he realized what had happened, he rushed to protect his most valuable assets. He sold the American Museum's collections to his manager and put both the museum building and Iranistan, plus several other pieces of real estate, in Charity's name. He used his available cash to settle his personal debts, then he and his East Bridgeport real estate company declared bankruptcy.

The news of the great P. T.'s downfall brought nothing but cheers from his enemies. They regarded it as poetic justice that the Prince of Humbugs had finally been humbugged himself—especially after all the boasting he had done in his autobiography.

Fortunately, P. T. Barnum had more friends than enemies. His financial problems prompted an outpouring of public sympathy. Several of his friends wanted to put up the money to bail him out, and total strangers wrote to offer their help.

Barnum turned them all down. He had placed enough assets in Charity's name to keep his family going until he could get back on his feet. "Without Charity, I am nothing," he declared, playfully quoting St. Paul.

Nevertheless, the Barnums were forced to leave Iranistan. They rented a smaller house in New York and took in boarders to provide them with an income. As a side effect of his reduced circumstances, P. T. gave up smoking. He could no longer afford his usual quota of ten cigars a day.

For perhaps the first and only time in his life, Phineas T. Barnum became depressed. The ordeal took an even greater toll on Charity. She developed an assortment of ailments that resisted all cures and remained a semi-invalid for the rest of her life.

In an effort to restore Charity's health, Barnum rented a summer house in Westhampton, Long Island.

He may have temporarily lost his money and his high spirits, but he had not lost his showman's instincts. While strolling along the beach one day, he found the body of a twelve-foot-long black whale that had recently washed ashore. Barnum had it shipped to the American Museum, where it was placed in a refrigerated showcase and exhibited for several days. He received a cut of the profits from the exhibit that nicely covered the expense of his family's summer vacation.

Barnum soon regained his normally optimistic outlook on life and even managed to find a ray of sunshine in the situation. "Last summer, in my poverty & seclusion at the sea-side with my family," he wrote to a friend, "I found more peace & contentment than Iranistan ever afforded me — & even on the Atlantic & this side of it, hope & happiness have been and are my handmaidens. All praise to Him for permitting me always to look upon the bright side of things."

Despite the fact that Barnum was living in sorely reduced circumstances, the holders of the bank notes he had signed for the Jerome Clock Company were convinced that he had money stashed away somewhere. He was hounded by lawyers. Some represented clients who had already been paid but were taking advantage of the showman's tangled finances to try to collect a second time.

Barnum was eager to put the clock company disaster behind him and make a start toward rebuilding his fortune, but first he had to get rid of his creditors. He began with a public announcement that he was all washed up. With half a million dollars' worth of debt hanging over his head, he said, he didn't see how he could possibly make a comeback. If his creditors were smart, they would settle for a percentage of what he owed them and not waste their time and money dunning him for the full amount. Barnum's statements were so convincing that his creditors agreed to a settlement. Half of his problem was solved.

But after publicly announcing that he was too depressed to work, the showman could hardly turn around and resume his career. Even if he claimed to have made a miraculous recovery, his creditors would find out and go after him again.

The only way to get back into show business, he decided, was to do it by stealth. In the winter of 1856, P. T. Barnum sailed for London. By coincidence, Mr. and Mrs. George C. Howard and their daughter Cordelia were on the same ship. A family of actors, the Howards were famous for their presentation of *Uncle Tom's Cabin* with Cordelia playing Little Eva.

Although P. T. Barnum's connection with the Howards was never mentioned, he looked up some of his old theatrical cronies in London and the family was soon performing in a theater in the West End. He kept an equally low profile when General Tom Thumb arrived shortly after New Year's to begin a European tour. Although he was now eighteen years old, the General was no more than an inch or two taller. Clearly, he was in no danger of losing his standing as a man in miniature.

As soon as Barnum found a place to live, he sent for Charity to join him. In the course of the next few years, she made several trips back and forth, and in the fall of 1857, Barnum returned to New York for a two-month stay. The occasion was the wedding of his second daughter, Helen, which took place at the home of her sister, Caroline, who was already married and living in Fairfield.

While they were in the neighborhood, Charity and P. T. dropped by to see how things were going at Iranistan. The mansion had been standing vacant ever since Barnum went bankrupt. He had hoped to sell it but no buyer had appeared, so the Barnums decided to move back in. A team of painters and carpenters had been hired to get the place ready for their return.

In the interim, Barnum and Charity had given up their rented house and were staying at a hotel in New York. One evening, about a week before Christmas, Barnum received a telegram from his half brother Philo informing him that Iranistan had been destroyed by fire. It was not clear how the blaze had started, but it was thought that one of the workmen may have dropped his lighted pipe onto the circular sofa in the central dome.

Thanks to fast action on the part of the fire fighters, most of the furnishings were saved. But the mansion itself was completely destroyed. To make matters worse, although the house was worth at least $150,000, Barnum had let several of his insurance policies lapse, so he was able to collect only about $28,000.

The showman took the news calmly. He never lost his head in a crisis. There had been another fire at Iranistan a few years earlier that broke out just a few hours before his daughter Caroline's wedding. Her husband-to-be, David Thompson, rushed off to tell Barnum, who was at the barbershop getting a shave.

"Never mind!" Barnum exclaimed. "We can't help these things; the house will probably be burned; but if no one is killed or injured, you shall be married tonight, if we are obliged to perform the ceremony in the coach house."

Miraculously, the fire was extinguished before it caused any serious damage and the wedding took place as scheduled. But Barnum's reaction to David Thompson's report of the blaze was typical. The instant he heard bad news, he was already working on a plan to salvage the situation.

The land on which Iranistan stood was subsequently sold to Elias Howe, the inventor of the sewing machine. He had planned to erect a mansion of his own, but he died suddenly and his plan was never carried out. The $50,000 from the sale of the property to Howe and the $28,000 worth of insurance went to pay off Barnum's clock company debts. Most of the money Barnum made in London had to be sent back to Connecticut for the same reason.

The showman was impatient with the process. He

wanted to be free of debt so he could start working toward amassing another fortune. When he returned to England several months after the fire at Iranistan, he decided to increase his income by taking to the lecture platform. Lectures were a major form of entertainment in that era, and good public speakers were always in demand. P. T.'s London friends encouraged him in the idea and even suggested a topic for him: "The Art of Money-Getting."

Barnum was dubious. "I told my friends that, considering my clock complications, I thought I was more competent to speak on 'The Art of Money-Losing,' " he wrote in his autobiography, "But they encouraged me by reminding me that I could not have lost money if I had not previously possessed the faculty of making it."

Barnum had no trouble lining up lecture dates. He was still a celebrity, and the public was eager to get a look at him. As it turned out, they also liked what he had to say. His lectures were very much like Barnum himself—a combination of entertainment and education. There were plenty of jokes and funny stories, but they were interspersed with serious comments on the virtues of thrift, perseverance, good manners, and hard work.

Barnum's work as a lecturer provided him with a substantial income and restored his hopes of making a financial comeback. For the next two years, he and Charity divided their time between Europe and America. He devoted part of his time to lecturing and part to managing Tom Thumb. Meanwhile, he was busy scout-

An advertising poster printed around 1881. It was designed to promote the circus but its main focus was P. T. Barnum. The boastful style leaves little doubt that it was written by the showman himself. (*Courtesy of Barnum Museum, Bridgeport, Connecticut*)

ing for new performers and exhibits, and quietly making plans to buy back the American Museum.

In March 1860, five years after he had gone into bankruptcy, P. T. Barnum regained control of his old stamping ground. He celebrated the event by taking out ads in all the newspapers and inundating New York with posters and placards announcing the good news: "Barnum on his feet again."

A gala celebration was held on his first day back on the job. The American Museum was festooned with an unusually large number of flags and banners, and hundreds of well-wishers crowded into the Lecture Room. P. T. Barnum stepped on stage and thanked his family and his friends for standing by him during his difficulties. His long ordeal was finally over. Now he was back in business, ready to take on the world, and his beloved American Museum was going to be bigger and better than ever.

Up in Smoke

After five years of living in rented houses and hotels, the Barnums were anxious to settle into a home of their own. Within a few months of resuming his ownership of the American Museum, Barnum built a house in Fairfield not far from where Iranistan had stood.

The Barnums' new home was a comfortable mansion set amid six acres of grounds. It was not as showy as its predecessor. Even its name was less pretentious, Lindencroft, after the handsome grove of linden trees that stood on one section of the property.

Not far away, the city of East Bridgeport, which had led to Barnum's financial woes, had fulfilled his expectations and become a thriving community. Several large factories had been erected there and homes were built for the employees—large, expensive ones for the owners and managers, and smaller, cheaper models for the laborers and mechanics.

Although he was gratified by the success of his real estate venture, Barnum's main interest now was in living up to his promise to make the American Museum bigger and better than ever. Among his new exhibits was a pair of white whales captured off the coast of Labrador. They were housed in a large tank filled with salt water that was installed on the second floor. A second tank in the basement became home to the first hippopotamus ever seen in the United States.

Barnum never claimed to be an expert in natural history. On the contrary, he often joked that he didn't know a clam from a codfish. In reality, he had an extensive knowledge of zoology and regularly exchanged theories and observations about animal behavior with such well-known scientists as Professor Louis Agassiz of Harvard University, who founded the American Museum of Natural History, and Spencer F. Baird, Secretary of the Smithsonian Institution.

In addition to fulfilling a personal interest, exhibiting wild animals was a surefire way to make money. A month after his return to the American Museum, Barnum engaged a western hunter and trapper named Grizzly Adams who had a menagerie that consisted of some two dozen grizzly bears plus lions, tigers, buffalo, and elk. Barnum presented the show in a huge tent on the Bowery and publicized it with a parade led by Adams in

his hunting outfit riding on the back of the largest grizzly bear.

After the fortune he had made with Tom Thumb,
P. T. was eager to find another midget. The General was
so rich by now that he was not particularly interested in
returning to the stage. He lived with his parents in a
splendid house in Bridgeport with his own separate
apartment scaled to his size.

Barnum's agents soon found him another man in
miniature. His name was George Washington Morrison
Nutt. Twelve years old and only twenty-nine inches tall,
the boy was already touring the country under the management of a second-rate showman. Barnum persuaded
his father, a New Hampshire farmer named Rodnia
Nutt, to sign a contract with him. It provided for
George's older and slightly taller brother, twenty-one-
year-old Rodnia, Jr., to accompany George on his tours.
Barnum agreed to pay both sons' room, board, clothing,
travel, and medical expenses and to see that they were
properly trained and educated.

Having made Tom Thumb a general, Barnum made
George Washington Morrison Nutt a commodore.
Adopting another policy that had been successful with
Tom, he ordered a miniature carriage for the boy.
Carved in the shape of a walnut, the top half of the shell
was hinged so it could be opened to reveal the Nutt in-
side. There was a Nutt on the outside, too. Four-foot-
tall Rodnia, Jr., served as his brother's coachman.

Not long after he discovered Commodore Nutt,

Barnum came across another midget, twenty-one-year-old Mercy Lavinia Warren Bump. He shortened the young woman's name to Lavinia Warren, dressed her in beautiful clothes and jewelry, and billed her as the "Queen of Beauty."

Tom Thumb, who was in the habit of visiting Barnum's Museum from time to time, saw the Queen of Beauty and fell in love with her on the spot. He all but abandoned his estate in Bridgeport and began spending most of his time at the home of his married sister in New York.

When Tom and Lavinia became better acquainted, he prevailed upon Barnum to invite her to Lindencroft for the weekend. The General met her at the train station, and after dropping her luggage at Barnum's, he gave her an extensive tour of his own property and introduced her to his parents. Tom joined the Barnums for dinner that evening, and later, when he and Lavinia were alone in the parlor, he asked her to become his wife. To his great delight, Lavinia agreed.

When their engagement was announced to the public, Tom joined Lavinia in her appearances at the museum. Thousands of people showed up to see the happy couple, and ticket sales regularly totaled $3,000 a day. Several of Barnum's business associates wanted him to hold the wedding at the Academy of Music, New York's leading opera house, and charge admission, but Barnum, who was rarely averse to making money, wouldn't hear of it. He had offered to pay for Tom and Lavinia's wedding and had promised to make it a dignified and tasteful occasion. He had no intention of breaking his word.

The Fairy Wedding, as the press called the event, took place on February 10, 1863. The ceremony was performed at fashionable Grace Church on Broadway and Tenth Street. George Washington Nutt served as Tom's best man, and Lavinia's sister, Minnie, who was even tinier than she was, was her maid of honor.

The wedding was followed by a reception for 2,000 people at the elegant Metropolitan Hotel. The guest list included Astors and Vanderbilts, several governors, senators and congressmen, and one or two Civil War generals. President and Mrs. Abraham Lincoln could not attend, but they presented the couple with a set of Chinese fire screens as a wedding gift and entertained the Thumbs at the White House when they passed through Washington on their wedding trip.

Although he had steadfastly refused to turn the Fairy Wedding into a sideshow, Barnum could not resist getting some mileage out of it. When Tom and Lavinia returned from their honeymoon, he sent the entire bridal party on a tour that took them all over the United States and Europe. In 1869, they made a trip around the world. It lasted three years and included performances in Japan, China, Australia, India, and Egypt.

The Fairy Wedding took place in the midst of the Civil War. Despite his preoccupation with the entertainment business, Barnum followed the struggle and the events that led up to it with keen interest. In his younger

The Fairy Wedding party in a portrait by the famous photographer, Matthew Brady. Barnum was often suspected of instigating the romance between Tom Thumb and Lavinia Warren, but for once he was innocent. (*Courtesy of Barnum Museum, Bridgeport, Connecticut*)

General and Mrs. Tom Thumb at their wedding reception. The picture shows the newlyweds standing on top of a piano to greet their guests. (*Courtesy of Barnum Museum, Bridgeport, Connecticut*)

years he had been a staunch Democrat, but as the party became more and more identified with secession and slavery, he switched his allegiance to the Republicans.

Although he was too old to serve in the army, Barnum paid the wages of four volunteer soldiers, a common practice in those days. He also contributed heavily to the Union cause. He was such an outspoken foe of the South that, more than once, an armed guard was posted at Lindencroft to protect him from Confederate assassins. When a group of Rebel agents arrived in New York in 1864 with orders to burn the city, the American Museum was high on their list of targets. Fortunately, they were intercepted before they could carry out their plan.

P. T. Barnum's detestation of slavery was so strong that he decided to run for the Connecticut General Assembly. If he was elected, he would have the honor of voting for the Thirteenth Amendment to the Constitution, which would abolish the practice for all time. He ran in the election of 1865 and won handily.

Fulfilling his hopes, the showman cast a yea vote for the ratification of the Thirteenth Amendment. Not content with that victory, he took the cause of civil rights a step further by urging the General Assembly to amend the state constitution to give blacks the vote. The legislators were reluctant to make such a move, but P. T. Barnum's stirring speech on the subject was reported in newspapers around the country.

Four years later the legislators relented. By then they had no choice. The Fifteenth Amendment to the

United States Constitution, granting blacks the right to vote, had already been ratified by two-thirds of the states. The clause in Connecticut's constitution barring them from the polls was both obsolete and illegal.

P. T. Barnum proved to be a capable and dedicated public servant. With no more battles to fight on the slavery front, he squared off against the railroad interests. The owners of the nation's biggest railroads were paying off politicians in an effort to gain control of all the rail lines in Connecticut. Once they got a monopoly, they could jack up the fares and the passengers would be forced to pay them.

Barnum regularly took the floor of the Assembly to condemn the railroad lobby and the legislators they paid off. He also introduced a bill that would protect railroad users from unreasonable fare hikes. One day in the summer of 1865, he was in the midst of delivering an eloquent speech on behalf of his bill when an aide handed him a telegram.

Barnum glanced at the message, laid it on his desk, and returned to his speech. Only later, when his bill had been voted on and passed, did he reveal the contents of the telegram. It was from his daughter Helen's husband, Samuel Hurd, informing him that the American Museum had burned down.

Barnum immediately rushed to New York, where he heard all the details. The fire had started in the museum's engine room and quickly spread through the huge building. Several people were injured in the rush

The burning of the American Museum, July 13, 1865. Fires destroyed two of Barnum's museums, one of his homes, his Hippotheatron arena, and the circus's winter quarters in Bridgeport. (*Courtesy of Barnum Museum, Bridgeport, Connecticut*)

for the exits, but luckily no one was killed. The bad news was that the museum and its collections were completely destroyed.

In the wake of the disaster, Barnum considered retiring from the museum business. He was fifty-five years old. He didn't have to work. He had more than enough money to live on for the rest of his life. After thinking it over, however, he changed his mind. If the establishment did not reopen, several hundred employees would be left without jobs and New York City would be left without a good museum. Perhaps more to the point, P. T. Barnum would run the risk of being bored to death.

Barnum found new quarters for his museum at Broadway and Spring Street, about twenty blocks north of the old location. He hired a team of agents to find a new set of exhibits and replaced the wild animals that had perished in the fire by merging with the Van Amburgh Menagerie Company, a first-class privately owned zoo. On November 13, 1865—exactly four months to the day since the fire—Barnum's New American Museum opened its doors.

Although it took a great deal of time to get the new museum up and running, Barnum did not neglect his duties as a state legislator. He continued to divide his time between New York and Hartford, and did so well in his first term in the Connecticut General Assembly that he was easily elected to a second.

Buoyed by his success, he decided to run for higher office. In 1867, he became the Republican candidate for

Congress from Connecticut's Fourth Congressional District. By coincidence, his opponent was also named Barnum—William H., a distant relative.

P. T. waged a vigorous campaign, but William H. had the upper hand from the start. Connecticut voters tended to be moralistic, and despite Barnum's excellent record in the Assembly, there was a general feeling that a man who made his living entertaining the public could not be trusted in a higher office.

William H. Barnum and his Democratic supporters capitalized on this feeling. They never missed a chance to remind the public of Joice Heth, the Fejee Mermaid, and Colonel John Fremont's Woolly Horse. Barnum was portrayed as a liar and a scoundrel, and by the end of the campaign, even some of his fellow Republicans had turned against him. He lost the race by nearly one thousand votes.

In his autobiography, the would-be congressman described himself as "neither disappointed or cast down" by his defeat. It may have been true. Perhaps it was merely a coincidence that for the next few years, he spent more time in New York than he did in Connecticut. He sold Lindencroft and bought a town house on Fifth Avenue and Thirty-ninth Street, only a few blocks from where the Crystal Palace had stood. The area was now a prime residential district.

For a man who liked to be on the go, New York was the perfect place. There was a constant round of dinner parties and receptions, visits to the opera and theater, and carriage rides through Central Park on Sunday afternoons. Barnum had a wide circle of friends that included the editor of the *New York Tribune*, Horace Greeley, the poets Alice and Phoebe Cary, and the famous Universalist preacher of the day, Edwin H. Chapin.

Chapin was the pastor of the Universalist Church Barnum attended in New York. He was an inveterate joker, just like his famous parishioner, and they thoroughly enjoyed each other's company. The two men spent so much time together that their friends called them Chang and Eng, after the famous Siamese Twins.

On the morning of March 3, 1868, Barnum was sitting at the breakfast table with Charity paging idly through the morning paper. Suddenly a headline caught his eye.

"Hallo!" he exclaimed. "Barnum's Museum has burned down."

Charity was puzzled. "I know," she replied. "It was totally destroyed two years ago, but you built another one."

"And that is burned," her husband told her as he proceeded to read the newspaper account of the blaze.

Charity was certain he was joking, but the more he read, the more she realized that the story was true. Charity was tremendously upset, but her husband, as usual, remained calm. According to the newspaper story, no one had been killed or injured. That was a relief. Barnum was saddened to think of the poor wild animals that had died in the fire, but there was nothing anyone could have done to save them. The blaze was already history. The question facing him at the moment was: What did the great P. T. plan to do next?

Rescued from Retirement

On the eve of his sixtieth birthday, Barnum wasn't sure that he felt up to starting a third American Museum. But if he abandoned the museum business, what was he going to do with the rest of his life?

His old friend, Horace Greeley, advised him to retire and "go a-fishing." Barnum was an avid fisherman. He owned a private lake in East Bridgeport where he often retreated with his rod and reel. But he wasn't interested in making fishing a full-time job. Instead, he became involved in building a new home.

Ever since they sold Lindencroft and moved to New York, the Barnums made it a practice to return to Connecticut for the summer. Charity's doctor thought the sea air might improve her health, so one summer they rented a house that was closer to Long Island Sound than any of their previous homes. They liked it so much that they decided to build a shorefront house of their own.

There was no need to search for a plot. Barnum already owned a substantial piece of beachfront property. A few years earlier, he had tried to persuade the city of Bridgeport to buy up a string of farms along Long Island Sound, clear the rocks from the beaches, and create a public park. When the city fathers refused, Barnum bought the land and built the park himself.

Seaside Park, as it was called, occupied only about half the property Barnum had purchased. The other half became the site of his new mansion. Waldemere—a name he coined by combining the German word for woods, *wald,* and the French word for sea, *mer*—was a rambling Victorian structure surrounded by gardens and fountains. When the master of the house was in residence, a silk banner with his initials, P.T.B., flew from the top of its cupola.

Since Seaside Park was more or less an extension of the Barnums' front yard, they often used it for clambakes and boating parties. But the park also became a popular recreation area for the residents of Bridgeport and nearby Fairfield. In addition to its long stretch of sandy beach and scenic water views, it had a merry-go-round and a bandstand, and several miles of winding roads that were perfect for a leisurely stroll or carriage ride.

While the carpenters and masons were hard at work

on Waldemere, Barnum resumed his career as a writer. He published a series of articles about famous frauds and hoaxes that appeared in *The New York Weekly Mercury* and later became a book, *The Humbugs of the World*. It was a perfect topic for a man who had often been branded a humbug himself. He also revised and expanded his autobiography, bringing out the new edition in 1869.

With those two projects behind him, he resurrected another career—lecturing. His speech on "The Art of Money-Getting" still drew large audiences. When it showed signs of growing stale, he replaced it with "The World and How to Live in It," which had a fresh collection of jokes and anecdotes but the same moral lessons.

P. T. Barnum's lecture tours took him all over the country. In several cities in the Midwest, he was introduced to people who had traveled miles to hear him. P. T. couldn't resist asking if they didn't really want to *see* him. An Iowa lady emphatically agreed. "Why, to tell you the truth, Mr. Barnum," she said, "we have read so much about you, and your museum and your queer carryings-on, that we were not quite sure but you had horns and cloven feet, and so we came to satisfy our curiosity; but la, me, I don't see but what you look a good deal like other folks, after all."

Although he had given up his museum, P. T. Barnum had not given up show business. In the fall of 1869, some workmen digging a well near the town of Cardiff in upstate New York discovered what was supposedly the fossilized body of a ten-foot-tall man. In reality, the object was a hoax perpetrated by a Binghamton cigar maker named George Hull.

The Cardiff Giant became a local tourist attraction and was eventually bought for $30,000 by a group of upstate businessmen. It was an enormous sum for that era, but the men expected to make many times that amount exhibiting the giant around the country.

Barnum happened to be in Albany when the Cardiff Giant went on display there. Realizing its potential as a moneymaker, he offered to buy the object. When its owners turned him down, he hired a local artist to make a miniature model of the giant. He then took the model to an artisan in New York who built a full-scale plaster replica, which Barnum exhibited himself.

This hoax of a hoax, as Barnum called it, attracted more viewers than the original Cardiff Giant and made its owners so angry that they applied for a court order to stop him from exhibiting it. The judge who heard the case was unmoved by their complaints. He could not help them, he said, unless the first Cardiff Giant appeared in court and testified that he was the only authentic giant.

With General Tom Thumb and his wedding party recently embarked on their three-year world tour, Barnum signed up another traveling troupe, among them the Siamese Twins, Chang and Eng Bunker. The Bunkers had been a stellar attraction ever since they arrived in the United States as teenagers some forty years earlier, but this was the first time they had worked for Barnum since their brief engagement at the American Museum a decade or so before. Nevertheless, it was Barnum who first called them the Siamese Twins, a name that subsequently became the accepted term for twins whose bodies do not fully separate.

By the winter of 1869, Barnum had run out of things to keep him busy. He was rescued from boredom by the arrival from England of an old friend named John Fish. The two had met in 1858 at one of Barnum's first lectures on "The Art of Money-Getting." Fish had read the first edition of the showman's autobiography a few years earlier and applied its principles, with the result that he had risen from working as a laborer in a cotton mill to owning a mill of his own. He attributed his success entirely to P. T. Barnum and became one of his most devoted admirers, even going so far as to name a pair of steam engines in his mill Barnum and Charity.

Barnum had spent many happy hours visiting with Fish and his family in England, so he was delighted when the mill owner finally took him up on his long-standing invitation to let him repay his hospitality in the United States. He arrived with his eldest daughter, and Barnum had a wonderful time escorting them around the country. They visited Niagara Falls, Mammoth Cave, New Orleans, Memphis, and a half-dozen other cities, including Washington, D.C., where they were received at the White House by President and Mrs. Ulysses S. Grant.

After a few months in New York, the trio set out on another lengthy jaunt. They traveled to California in a private car on the recently completed transcontinental railroad, but returned to spend the first half of the summer at Waldemere and the remaining half touring Canada.

During his tour of California, Barnum saw the sea lions playing at Seal Rocks in San Francisco and seriously considered bringing some back to New York and exhibiting them in a fenced-in area of the East River.

Although he abandoned that idea, he could not resist signing a contract to exhibit a new midget. The boy's name was Leopold Kahn and he was even tinier than Tom Thumb had been when Barnum first discovered him. Before sending him on tour, Barnum rechristened him "Admiral Dot."

In the fall of 1870, not long after John Fish and his daughter returned to England, P. T. Barnum entertained another pair of visitors. They came on business, not pleasure, and their visit was relatively brief. Their names were William C. Coup and Dan Castello, and they were the owners of the "Egyptian Caravan," the country's largest traveling circus.

Coup and Castello wanted the great P. T. to become a partner in the Egyptian Caravan. It was already very successful, but with his name, talent and financial resources behind it, there was no limit to how great it could be.

Barnum's family and friends were appalled that he would even consider Coup and Castello's proposition, but Barnum dismissed their objections. He was itching to go back to work.

The Greatest Show on Earth

The circus was a less than drastic departure from Barnum's previous activities. In many ways it was a logical next step. His museums had featured the same kinds of attractions that appeared in circus sideshows—midgets, giants, tattooed men, and bearded ladies. He knew how to assemble and care for a menagerie and he had a talent for lining up entertainment the public would pay to see.

The instant their partnership became official, Barnum hurled himself into expanding Coup and Castello's operations. Any circus that bore his name had to be as fabulous as he could possibly make it.

He contacted the dealers who had supplied him with wild animals for his museums and put together a more extensive menagerie. He contributed his two most lucrative exhibits, Admiral Dot and the Cardiff Giant, and found an impressive lineup of new ones, including Zazel, the human cannonball; a goat, Alexis, that could jump through hoops while riding around the ring on the back of a horse; a group of "four wild Fiji cannibals" whom one of his agents claimed to have ransomed from an enemy chieftain who was about to kill them; and Captain Djordji Costentenus, a "noble Greek" whose entire body was covered with tattoos. To forestall any suspicions that the tattoos might be painted on, Barnum had them authenticated by a group of prominent Boston physicians, including the renowned Dr. Oliver Wendell Holmes.

P. T. Barnum's Museum, Menagerie and Circus, as the new version of Coup and Castello's show was called, opened in Brooklyn, New York, on April 10, 1871. It was presented in a collection of huge tents that covered three acres and could hold as many as 10,000 spectators. The tents were not a new idea. Circuses used them because they were easy to transport, but this was the first time any circus had used three acres' worth.

After buying their tickets at the entrance, the patrons passed through a series of five medium-sized tents where the museum, menagerie, and sideshow exhibits were displayed. From there they entered the big top, where the show itself took place.

After a one-week stand in Brooklyn, the circus went on tour through New England and upper New York State. There was never a shortage of patrons. At one stop

116

in Waterville, Maine, so many people lined up to buy tickets that the troupe held continuous performances, starting in the early morning and continuing until nine at night.

It soon became obvious that there was one drawback to staging a circus in an oversize tent. The people in the back rows had a hard time seeing the show. The simplest solution was to enlarge the ring where the acts were performed, but another consideration made that out of the question.

The standard diameter for circus rings throughout the world had been set at thirteen meters, slightly under forty-three feet. Circus horses were trained to perform in rings of this size. If every circus had a different size, the horses would have to be retrained every time they appeared with a new company.

Barnum and his partners solved the problem by keeping the rings the same size but increasing their number. They started by adding a second ring and eventually expanded to the three rings that are the norm today. With the increase in the number of rings, however, the clowns' jokes and silly remarks could not be heard in the farthest reaches of the tent. As a result, another circus tradition was born. The clowns' dialogues were eliminated and they performed all their routines in pantomime.

P. T. Barnum's Museum, Menagerie and Circus was in business for only six months of the year. With the onset of cold weather, it became impossible to present the show outdoors under a tent. Disinclined as always to stop working, Barnum spent his winters looking for new acts and dreaming up ways to sell even more tickets when the circus resumed its operations in the spring.

One of his brainstorms during the first year's lull was to give the show a new and catchier name. The one he chose was "P. T. Barnum's Great Traveling Exposition and World's Fair, The Greatest Show on Earth." The second half of the name has endured to this day.

Back in the days when Barnum worked for Aaron Turner's Old Columbian Circus, anyone connected with a circus, or with any other branch of the entertainment business, was regarded as a dubious character. Barnum, a regular churchgoer and a devoted family man, had always resented the slur.

The circus became slightly more reputable during the years after the Civil War, but there were still some lingering doubts. In many communities, the local clergy preached sermons exhorting their congregations not to patronize it. Decent people often stayed away anyway. Traveling shows tended to attract pickpockets and con men, and were often associated with gambling and drunkenness.

Barnum set out to change this shady image. He banned the use of alcohol by his employees, kept a strict eye on security, and made sure that none of the acts contained any material that might offend the public's sense of decency. P. T. Barnum's circus was going to be noted for clean, wholesome family entertainment, and it was.

Barnum secured public testimonials from prominent clergymen attesting to the fact and endorsing its educational value as well.

William Coup and Dan Castello handled the day-to-day running of the show, while Barnum was in charge of promotion. He still had plenty of friends in the newspaper business, and they were happy to run the items he sent them. It was not just a matter of friendship, however. His stories were always eye-catching. Moreover, the circus, like Barnum's American Museum, always bought pages and pages of ads.

One of the great P. T.'s cleverest publicity ideas was born out of practical considerations. The circus traveled by train, and it was a major undertaking to unload the equipment and transport the entire company to the site where the tents would be set up.

Barnum conceived the idea of turning what had been a dreary chore into a festive occasion. The performers donned their costumes, the band put on their uniforms and unpacked their instruments, the elephants lumbered along beside their trainers, and the circus parade was born. In addition to solving the transportation problem, the event always drew a big crowd and made everyone eager to see the show.

Within the space of a single year, P. T. Barnum turned William Coup and Dan Castello's circus into a larger and more successful operation than it had been without him. It soon dawned on the partners, however, that there was a serious drawback to mounting a show of this size. It cost a small fortune to move the troupe from one place to another. The menagerie alone took up several dozen freight cars, and additional cars were needed to transport the circus wagons, carts, and chariots. Then there were the passenger fares. All told, the circus company—performers, roustabouts, ticket sellers, and managers—numbered several hundred people.

Concerned about the way transportation costs were eating into their profits, Coup and Castello began to have second thoughts about continuing the operation on such a gigantic scale. Economically, it would make more sense to work with a smaller show. Barnum wouldn't hear of it.

The only places where they actually lost money were small, out-of-the-way towns where they could never hope to sell more than a few hundred tickets. Barnum suggested that they bypass these whistle stops and play only in larger cities. The railroads could then run special excursion trains bringing the people from outlying towns to the circus, instead of letting the circus come to them.

The railroads, of course, were more than willing to cooperate in any venture that provided them with more riders. The revised system proved to be a boon for the circus, too. In 1872, the first year the new plan went into operation, the Greatest Show on Earth made over a million dollars, more than twice as much as it had made the year before.

One of the brightest stars of the show was P. T.

Barnum himself. Many people considered it worth the price of admission just to get a look at the world-famous showman. Barnum was happy to oblige. At every performance, he would drive around the arena in a carriage, stopping every few yards to announce, "You came to see Barnum? Well, I'm Barnum."

He also used the circus as a vehicle for selling copies of his autobiography. He had already written two versions, one in 1855 and another in 1869, and he continued to bring out new editions—and to display and sell them at the circus—for the rest of his life.

With his eye as always on the bottom line, Barnum started hatching plans to make the circus a year-round operation. It didn't make sense to put together a show that operated for only six months of the year, particularly when it cost money to store the equipment and feed and care for the menagerie during the winter.

At the end of the 1872 season, Barnum bought and renovated a large arena, the Hippotheatron, on Broadway and Fourteenth Street in New York. There he planned to present some of the choicest acts from the Greatest Show on Earth during the winter months.

The company was installed at the Hippotheatron and Barnum took off for New Orleans, where he was producing another version of the circus. On Christmas Eve, he received a telegram from his manager, Samuel Hurd. Earlier that morning, the Hippotheatron had burned to the ground.

As in the previous fires at Iranistan and the American Museums, no one was killed or seriously injured. The worst casualties of the blaze were the animals. The lions' and tigers' cages were too heavy to move, and the firemen, afraid of turning wild animals loose in the streets, did not set them free. Four giraffes might have been saved, but they were so paralyzed by fright that they refused to leave the building. When the flames died down, all that remained of Barnum's magnificent menagerie were two elephants and a camel.

The rest of the circus was equally decimated. Props and scenery were burned, the musicians lost their instruments and uniforms, and the performers' costumes were a total loss.

William Coup and Dan Castello were devastated by the disaster. In show business, the week after Christmas was the busiest time of the year. In addition to losing the holiday crowds, they would be unable to send the circus out on the road in the spring. There was no way they could assemble a new show that soon. The only alternative was to close down for a year.

P. T. Barnum emphatically disagreed with his partner's gloomy pronouncement. What nonsense! They were not completely wiped out. Their tents, chariots, and wagons had survived. The only thing they needed to salvage the situation was energy, courage, pluck, and money.

He fired off a cable to his London agent instructing

him to purchase an array of new attractions and find a new menagerie. He ordered a collection of new exhibits for the museum section of the show. In a matter of three short months, the circus was reconstituted and the Greatest Show on Earth opened on schedule the following spring.

Barnum and Bailey

In the summer of 1873, while P. T. Barnum's Museum, Menagerie and Circus was following its usual route around the country, its namesake was making plans to tour Europe. He was talking about financing a balloon expedition across the Atlantic Ocean, and he wanted to discuss the project with some French and British balloon experts.

As usual Charity stayed at home, but this time there was not even a suggestion that she might join him later on. She had been ill for the past two years with a serious heart condition and rarely strayed far from Waldemere.

Barnum sailed for Europe in the fall of 1873. His first stop was Liverpool, where his old friend John Fish met him at the dock and whisked him off to his estate in nearby Southport. After a few days' visit with the

Fishes, Barnum went on to London and from there to Germany, Austria, and Czechoslovakia. His interest in ballooning faded, but he did visit every zoo, museum, and circus he could find. In Hamburg, he finally had a chance to meet Carl Hagenback, Europe's foremost animal supplier, with whom he had been doing business for years.

Hagenback was a walking encyclopedia of animal acts, and Barnum, always in the market for innovative ideas, spent days picking his brain. Hagenback told him about the Indian sport of elephant racing and suggested that ostrich races might be another good idea. Barnum took copious notes, and Hagenback was amply repaid with an order for $15,000 worth of animals. The ostrich races eventually showed up in the circus, with fake monkeys as jockeys instead of the live ones Hagenback had proposed.

Barnum had finished his business in Hamburg and was preparing to leave for Holland when a cable arrived from home. Charity was dead.

Her death was a double tragedy for Barnum. In addition to losing his wife of forty-four years, he had been thousands of miles away when she died. Worse yet, there was no possibility of getting home in time for her funeral.

The bereaved husband cabled instructions for the service and requested that Charity's casket be placed in a vault in Mountain Grove cemetery until he could return to Bridgeport for her burial. Then he closeted himself in his hotel room and spent the next few days in tears and prayers.

In the aftermath of Charity's death, Barnum began to feel ill himself. He suffered from recurring headaches and dizziness, which became so severe that he abandoned his plans to visit Holland and returned to England to recuperate.

During his travels abroad, Barnum kept in close touch with his business interests in New York. Having rebuilt his fire-damaged circus, he was now working on a replacement for the devastated Hippotheatron. He had bought a large plot of land on Madison Avenue and Twenty-seventh Street and was planning to build a mammoth arena that would be called the Great Roman Hippodrome. In addition to providing spacious quarters for a museum, menagerie, and aquarium, the arena was designed to seat 12,000 spectators.

According to the reports he received from William Coup and Dan Castello, the Great Roman Hippodrome was almost finished. Barnum had already decided to open his first show with an immense parade called "The Congress of Nations." The parade would feature elephants and camels, gilded chariots, horses draped in splendid fabrics, and a sea of multicolored flags and banners representing every imaginable nation. The members of the circus cast would impersonate the "Kings, Queens, Emperors and other potentates of the civilized world," wearing appropriately opulent costumes for their roles.

The idea was not original. Barnum borrowed it from a pair of English showmen, George and John Sanger. Far from objecting to his duplication of their spectacle, the Sangers sold him their chariots and costumes to use in the American version.

Magnificent processions like the Congress of Nations became the standard opening for every Barnum circus. They often included as many as a thousand marchers. The themes changed from year to year. One year the parade re-created a Chinese emperor's court, complete with lantern bearers, flame throwers, and Tartar cavalrymen. The Hippodrome was built to accommodate such elaborate production numbers. Barnum thought nothing of re-creating an English stag hunt, for example, with 150 riders in formal hunting costumes pursuing thirty-six live stags.

The opening of the Hippodrome revived Barnum's interest in balloon flight. He enlisted Professor Washington H. Donaldson, a serious researcher in the field, to make regularly scheduled ascensions taking along various instruments with which to measure air currents and altitudes. It is not clear whether the professor's findings were useful, but the sight of a huge balloon flying over Manhattan Island was a superb ad for the Hippodrome. When the circus went on the road that year, Professor Donaldson and his balloon went along.

Within a year after Charity's death, Barnum remarried. His bride was twenty-four-year-old Nancy Fish, the youngest daughter of his English friend John Fish.

Nancy was forty years younger than her sixty-four-year-old bridegroom and seventeen years younger than his oldest daughter. The marriage caused some tension in the family, but eventually, Barnum's daughters became reconciled to the match and even Charity's relatives accepted it. Nancy became Aunt Nancy to Barnum's numerous grandchildren.

The second Mrs. Barnum was a sharp contrast to the ailing, homebound woman Charity had become in her later years. She enjoyed entertaining, shared her husband's love of the theater and opera, and was always ready to accompany him on his travels. The newlyweds spent part of each winter in New York, and in the summer they visited such fashionable resorts as Newport, Block Island, the Adirondacks, and the White Mountains.

Much as he enjoyed gadding about the country and the world, Barnum still considered Bridgeport home. When a group of local politicians urged him to run for mayor of his adopted city, he did not have to think twice about saying yes.

In the years after the Civil War, Bridgeport had become a predominantly Democratic city. P. T. Barnum was one of the few Republicans elected that year, and he won by an impressive majority. When the results were announced around midnight on April 5, 1875, a parade of his supporters marched down to Waldemere. They brought along a brass band, and after a rousing rendition of "Hail to the Chief," His Honor acknowledged their cheers and shouts with a short speech of thanks and a few jokes about his "youthfulness" for the office. He was sixty-five years old.

Barnum proved to be an excellent mayor. One of his major contributions to the city was persuading the local water company to enlarge its reservoir and upgrade its purification system so that Bridgeport and its neighboring towns could be assured of a constant supply of clean water. He also saved the taxpayers money by instituting a policy of competitive bidding for the contract to supply the gas for the city's streetlights. He was less successful, however, in one of his other attempts to reduce the municipal budget. The Democrats on the Common Council consistently voted down his efforts to give them a fifteen-percent pay cut.

The mayor's term of office was one year, which was quite enough for Barnum. He had no desire to run for reelection. As a businessman, he was used to doing things his own way. He disliked having to get the approval of the Common Council before making a move, and it galled him to see some of his most sensible plans for civic improvement voted down.

Despite their frequent disagreements, Barnum ended his association with the Common Council on a friendly note. At their final session, he placed flowers on each of the councilmen's desks. Then he delivered a farewell speech in which he noted that they would now fold their tents like the Arabs and silently steal away, but they could take pride in the fact that this was "the only 'stealing' which was performed by this Honorable Body" during his administration.

One of Barnum's happiest jobs as mayor was ushering in America's centennial in 1876. He ordered all the church bells in Bridgeport rung at midnight to celebrate the beginning of that momentous year. The occasion seemed made to order for P. T. Barnum. He pulled out all the stops, putting together a traveling show that presented, as he described it, "a real old-fashioned Yankee-Doodle, Hail-Columbia, Fourth-of-July celebration every day."

The show opened with a thirteen-gun salute and included a huge parade with marchers in Revolutionary War uniforms, a man dressed as General George Washington astride a white horse, and a young woman dressed as the Goddess of Liberty. A chorus of several hundred voices sang patriotic songs, and at night there was a colossal fireworks display with skyrockets forming eagles and flags, and spelling out the years 1776 and 1876.

Barnum considered taking the show to Europe and opening it there in the fall of 1877, but he never carried out his plan. That spring, his youngest and favorite daughter, Pauline, died of diphtheria at the age of thirty-one, leaving behind a heartbroken husband and two young sons. Barnum put aside his business interests for a few weeks and went off to Europe with Nancy to recover from his sorrow.

P. T. Barnum may have had his fill of being mayor,

but he was not ready to give up politics completely. In 1877, he again ran for the Connecticut General Assembly and was elected for two terms. When he left office, he continued his public service in other ways.

He used part of his large fortune to build the Bridgeport Public Library. He donated money to establish the Bridgeport Hospital and endowed the Barnum Museum of Natural History at Tufts College in Medford, Massachusetts. The college was a particular favorite because it had been founded under Universalist auspices.

In spite of his many other interests, Barnum was still very much involved with his circus. He had severed his association with William Coup and Dan Castello and was working with a new team of partners. The show was as successful as ever, but it had plenty of competitors. Most of the rival circus owners were younger men, and Barnum began to have doubts about his ability to keep up with them.

The show that posed the most serious threat was the Great London Circus, Sanger's Royal British Menagerie and Grand International Allied Shows—an amalgamation of three different companies that was owned by an English showman, James A. Bailey.

An efficient and talented manager as well as a hardheaded businessman, Bailey was Barnum's match when it came to getting publicity. In the course of one of their tours, an elephant in the Great London Circus's menagerie gave birth to the first baby elephant conceived and born in America. Barnum immediately contacted Bailey and offered to buy Columbia, as the elephant was called, for $100,000. Bailey refused, then turned around and publicized the offer so the public could appreciate the baby elephant's value.

After that experience, Barnum decided that James A. Bailey was precisely the kind of man he wanted as his partner. Bailey agreed to the deal, and in the summer of 1880 his show became P. T. Barnum's Greatest Show on Earth, Sanger's Royal British Menagerie, The Great London Circus and Grand International Allied Shows.

Its stars included such perennial crowd-pleasers as the original Fejee Mermaid and General and Mrs. Tom Thumb. The General, who lived in semiretirement at his Bridgeport estate, had grown stout in his middle age, but he and Lavinia had not forgotten how to entertain an audience.

One of the results of Barnum's new partnership was that James A. Bailey's circus gave up its winter quarters in Philadelphia and moved to Bridgeport. Barnum set aside a twelve-acre plot along the tracks of the New York, New Haven and Hartford Railroad—the very site where he had once startled passengers with the sight of an elephant hitched to a plow. He built special steam-heated, temperature-controlled buildings for the wild animals and a stable that could hold several hundred horses. A series of sheds housed the circus wagons, tents, and other equipment. All the buildings were decorated with flags, and there were brightly colored paintings of the animals and huge signs announcing the presence of the Greatest Show on Earth.

The performers, laborers, and other employees lived in the area during the winter months, and the local shopkeepers made a good living supplying their needs. Eight lines of track led from the circus quarters to the main railroad line, making it easy for the troupe to get on the road when spring arrived. In the meantime, the complex served as a living advertisement to rail passengers of the delights that awaited them when the season began.

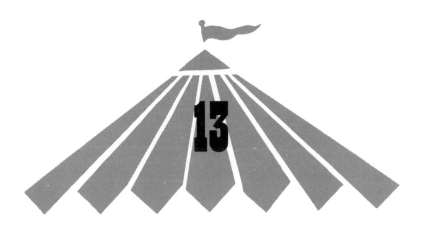

Jumbo

P. T. Barnum never stopped searching for new attractions for his circus. In 1880, he discovered another superstar—a six-and-a-half-ton, eleven-foot-tall African elephant named Jumbo. The elephant, the largest in captivity, belonged to the Royal Zoological Society and was one of the most popular inhabitants of London's Regent's Park Zoo. He was a special favorite of the children who, for twopence a ride, could perch in the howdah on his back and be carried around the park.

The zoo's superintendent had his own reasons for wanting to sell Jumbo. The animal had already become violent on two occasions, and the superintendent was afraid he might run amok and kill some of the children. When Barnum expressed an interest in buying the elephant, the superintendent quickly agreed.

Jumbo with his keeper, Matthew Scott. The elephant was the only member of the circus who was exempt from Barnum's ban on alcohol; his diet included a daily keg of beer. (*Courtesy of Barnum Museum, Bridgeport, Connecticut*)

The news of the purchase caused an uproar in England. Jumbo was a national institution. Nobody wanted to part with him, much less see him sold to an American. Even Jumbo resisted the idea. He refused to enter the oversize wagon that was sent to transport him to the dock. When an attempt was made to walk him there instead, the elephant balked at that too. He lay down in the street outside the zoo and resisted every effort to make him move.

Barnum's English agent sent him a cable demanding to know what to do with the stubborn pachyderm. P. T.'s reply was: "Let him lie there a week if he wants to. It is the best advertisement in the world."

By this time "Jumbomania" was rampant on both sides of the Atlantic. Pictures of the elephant were displayed on fans, jewelry, hats, prints, and trade cards. He was hailed in songs and poems and featured in ads for any number of products. He even began to receive fan mail.

The elephant could not lie in the middle of a London street indefinitely, however, and finally someone found the way to make him move. Jumbo's keeper, Matthew Scott, had been given the job of getting him to the dock, but it so happened that Scotty had a vested interest in having him stay at the zoo. He was allowed to keep the money he collected for the elephant rides. If Jumbo joined the circus, Scotty would lose a good chunk of his income.

When Barnum's agent became aware of this fact, he

invited the keeper to accompany Jumbo to the United States. He offered him a substantial salary and also arranged for his job at the zoo to be held open for him in case he disliked the United States and decided to return.

The very next day Jumbo docilely marched into the wagon drawn up beside his cage and ten horses pulled it to a London dock. A huge crowd gathered at the pier to see him off, and a party of aristocrats, including a baroness who was one of his most devoted fans, boarded the ship when it made its last stop at Gravesend and treated Jumbo to a final meal of English buns.

When the ship arrived in New York thirteen days later, Barnum and his partners, along with a horde of reporters, were on hand to welcome Jumbo. It took sixteen horses and several hundred men to drag the crate he traveled in to Madison Square Garden (the Great Roman Hippodrome's new name), where the circus had opened a few weeks earlier.

P. T. Barnum spent $30,000 to buy Jumbo and ship him to New York, but he earned it back within days of his arrival. People flocked to see "The Largest and Noblest Animal on the Face of the Earth." Jumbo did not perform, because he had never been trained to do tricks, but he and Scotty resumed their routine of selling rides on his back.

For the next four seasons, Jumbo was the shining star of Barnum and Bailey's circus. He was just as beloved in America as he had been in England. Contrary to the Regent's Park Zoo superintendent's fears, he never went berserk and injured anyone; but when he was feeling rambunctious he sometimes broke down the stone walls of his pen.

In September 1885, the circus was touring Canada. They had finished a performance in St. Thomas, Ontario, and Jumbo and the other elephants were being led down some railroad tracks to be put aboard the train that would take them to their next stop. Suddenly, a freight train running off schedule came roaring down the tracks. The elephant handlers tried to herd their charges down a steep embankment to get them out of its way, but Jumbo refused to go. He raised his enormous head, trumpeted loudly, and went charging off down the track. The engine struck him from behind, fracturing his skull and causing massive internal injuries. He died within minutes, with his old friend Scotty sobbing at his side.

Even in death, Jumbo became a hero. The newspapers reported that he had died saving the dwarf elephant, Tom Thumb, who was grazed by the engine but suffered only a broken leg.

From the minute he bought Jumbo, P. T. Barnum had been concerned that some type of accident might claim the life of his prize elephant. He had already arranged with a taxidermist to salvage and mount Jumbo's hide and skeleton in the event of a catastrophe. Both the Smithsonian Institution in Washington and the American Museum of Natural History in New York were eager to acquire them. But Barnum had other plans.

The mounted elephant continued to travel with the circus for the next three years. He was exhibited beside Alice, another import from the Regent's Park Zoo, who was described as his widow. When interest waned, Barnum sent Jumbo's skeleton to the American Museum of Natural History, where it remains to this day. The hide went to the Barnum Museum of Natural History at Tufts College, but was destroyed when the museum burned down in 1975.

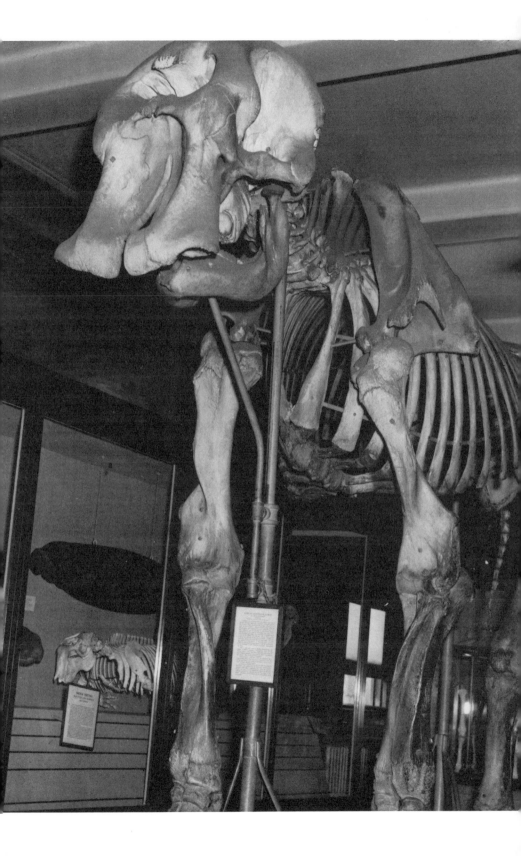

Barnum continued to make money out of Jumbo even after his death. *Left:* Jumbo's skeleton. (*Neg. no. 2A 2436 Courtesy of Department of Library Services American Museum of Natural History*) *Above:* Barnum had Jumbo's hide mounted separately to create a new circus exhibit, "Double Jumbo." (*Courtesy of Tufts University Archives*)

The Show Is Over

P. T. Barnum's career was plagued by so many fires that he was occasionally accused of setting them himself as a publicity stunt. The accusation was untrue. No amount of publicity was worth the money and the headaches they cost him.

On November 20, 1887, yet another fire broke out. This one occurred at the Barnum and Bailey Circus's winter quarters in Bridgeport. There was no loss of human life, but again the entire menagerie was destroyed, including Jumbo's so-called widow, Alice. Barnum was in New York at the time, and when Nancy woke him with the news, he calmly turned over and went back to sleep. His unruffled response was typical, but his subsequent behavior was not.

Instead of leaping into action as he had in the past,

he let James A. Bailey order a new menagerie and supervise the show's recovery from the blaze. Shortly afterward, Barnum officially stepped aside and let Bailey take over. His only request was that he continue to be consulted on major decisions and allowed to offer friendly advice if and when he felt it was needed.

Now seventy-eight years of age, the old showman was still in remarkably good health. His much younger wife was not as fortunate. Within a few years of their marriage, she had developed almost as many ailments as Charity. From time to time she would take to her bed or check into some fashionable sanatorium for treatment.

Charity had often complained when P. T. went traveling without her. Nancy rarely objected. When he was invited to attend a Tufts College commencement and present an honorary degree to one of his old friends, for example, she insisted that he go. It didn't take much persuading. Barnum had never seen a college commencement, and he didn't want to miss this one. He made a speech at one of the commencement dinners and was serenaded by the college glee club with "The Barnum Song," a witty tune that had been composed in his honor.

During some of his other visits to Tufts, Barnum spent time in Boston posing for a marble bust to be placed in the Museum of Natural Science. The sculptor was Thomas Ball, whose works include the mounted statue of George Washington in the Boston Public Gar-

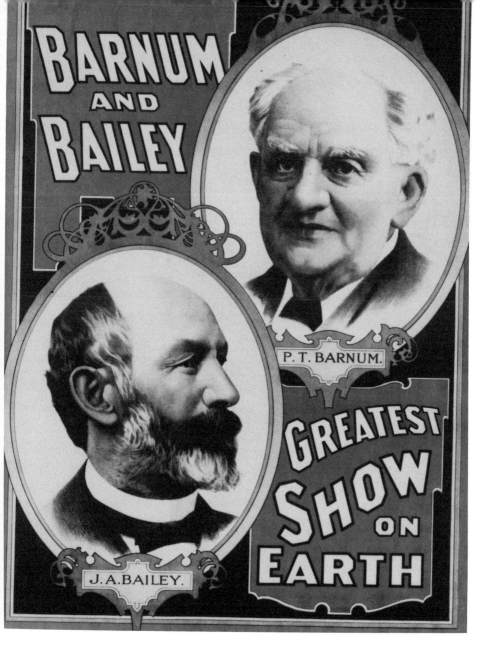

A poster advertising the Greatest Show on Earth. Barnum was close to eighty years old when this picture was taken. His partner, James A. Bailey, was thirty-seven years younger. (*Courtesy of Barnum Museum, Bridgeport, Connecticut*)

den and the statue of Daniel Webster in New York's Central Park.

When James A. Bailey and another circus partner, James L. Hutchinson, heard about the bust, they commissioned Ball to do a full-size bronze statue of Barnum. Using the cast for the bust and some photographs, the sculptor returned to his studio in Florence to execute the commission.

With uncharacteristic modesty, Barnum agreed to the statue on condition that it not be displayed during his lifetime. Even after his death, he told Ball, he couldn't imagine where it might be erected. "Perhaps my posterity and the public will wisely conclude to *bury* it," he said.

The statue was completed in 1886. After winning First Class honors at an International Exhibition in Munich, it was shipped to the United States and stored in a warehouse in Hoboken, New Jersey. A private unveiling was held for Barnum and his family and friends. Bailey and Hutchinson attended and pronounced it "the best-executed statue and the most perfect likeness we ever before saw." Then Barnum ordered the likeness to be returned to its crate and not taken out until he was "moldering in the grave."

Realizing that such an event might not be too far off, Barnum began to plan for Nancy's life as a widow. He knew she would not want to live in a mansion the size of Waldemere, so he decided to build a smaller house. The twenty acres of land on which Waldemere

The Barnum statue in Bridgeport's Seaside Park. In the background is the site of Barnum's last home, Marina, now the campus of the bankrupt University of Bridgeport. (*Courtesy of Corbit Studio, Bridgeport, Connecticut*)

stood was subdivided. A small colony of seaside villas was built on one half, and on the other, a new brick home, Marina.

After Barnum and Nancy held a farewell party for nine hundred guests at Waldemere, a wrecking crew arrived and tore it down. Seaside Park was deeded to the city of Bridgeport and the spacious oval that separated the house from the park became part of the package, with the proviso that the site remain open so that nothing would obstruct Nancy's view.

In spite of his advancing years, Barnum continued to have twice as much energy as his wife. Still one of Bridgeport's biggest boosters, he was a member of the city's Parks Commission, served on the board of the Pequonnock Bank, and was a director of the Bridgeport and Port Jefferson Steamboat Company, which is still in business and operates a ferry across Long Island Sound.

But the Greatest Show on Earth remained his pride and joy. He had always wanted to bring the circus to England, and in the fall of 1889, he finally managed to do it. The entire show was transported, including the deceased Jumbo, whose skeleton and hide were reunited for one last time. It played at the Olympia, London's largest exhibition hall, and was so popular that hundreds of would-be patrons had to be turned away at the door.

One of the most enthusiastic members of the audience was Queen Victoria's grandson, Prince George, who later became King George V. The Prince pronounced himself so pleased with the show that instead of staying for only part of it, as the royals often did, he was going to remain "until they sing 'God Save Grandmother.' "

P. T. and Nancy spent several months in England seeing old friends, visiting Nancy's family, and being interviewed by the press. Even in his old age, Barnum could never pass up an opportunity to get his name before the public. As he once told a reporter for the *New York Times*, "I don't care much what the papers say about me, provided they say something."

On their return from England, the Barnums took a trip to Colorado, where P. T.'s daughter Helen now lived. They arrived back in Bridgeport at the end of October. A week or so later, Barnum suffered a stroke. Although he seemed to be rallying, his heart was weak and the doctors held out little hope for his recovery. They urged Nancy not to tell him how sick he was, lest the news make him worse.

Barnum wasn't fooled. He sent for his lawyer and made some changes in his will. One of them was a bequest to Tufts College to enlarge his Museum of Natural History. There were other gifts to the Bridgeport Universalist Society, the Universalist Publishing House in Boston, the Bridgeport Scientific Society, and the Fairfield County Historical Society. He also left $50,000 to build the Barnum Institute of Science and History, approving the plans and signing the contracts for the building on his deathbed. The Institute, now called the

Barnum Museum, is appropriately devoted to exhibits about the circus, the city of Bridgeport, and its founder's career.

Barnum was confined to Marina and tended by private nurses, but he was able to get out of bed for part of each day. He remained as cheerful as ever, telling jokes, giving interviews to the press, and issuing orders about the arrangements for his funeral.

When the editor of *The New York Evening Sun* heard that he was wondering what his obituary would say, the paper obligingly published it for him. GREAT AND ONLY BARNUM, said the headline. "He Wanted To Read His Obituary; Here It Is." The write-up appeared on March 24, 1891, two days before the circus was scheduled to open at Madison Square Garden, but the *Sun* also reported—quite dishonestly—that Barnum was on the road to recovery.

On the evening of April 6, Barnum's condition became worse and it was clear that he did not have much longer to live. A little after six-thirty on the following evening, he died. At his funeral on April 10, the church was packed with mourners. Another throng stood outside, and more crowds waited along the route from the church to Mountain Grove Cemetery. Flags flew at half-mast, and practically every home and business in Bridgeport was draped with black. In New York, the circus canceled the day's performances as a tribute to their departed leader and the employees took the train to Bridgeport for the funeral.

149

Under the terms of P. T. Barnum's agreement with James A. Bailey, Barnum's estate was to receive a share of the profits from the Greatest Show on Earth for three years after his death. In 1894, it reverted to Bailey. After Bailey's death in 1906, the circus was sold to the Ringling Brothers, who continued to run it as a separate show until 1918. They then merged it with their own circus to become Ringling Brothers Barnum and Bailey Circus. Bridgeport remained the country's main "circus town" until 1927, when its winter quarters were transferred to Sarasota, Florida.

By the time P. T. Barnum died, he had earned the respect and affection of his fellow Americans. His escapades with Joice Heth and the Fejee Mermaid had been forgiven and largely forgotten. In the years after the Civil War, the country had shed many of its puritanical attitudes. Popular entertainment was no longer equated with sin, and the man who had almost single-handedly created it became something of a hero. Once denounced as the Prince of Humbugs, in his later years he was acclaimed as "The World's Greatest Showman."

Only one vestige of P. T. Barnum's earlier reputation remains. He is widely credited with saying, "There's a sucker born every minute," although all the evidence points to the fact that he never said it. The statement does not appear in any of his writings or in the extensive—and not always favorable—coverage he got in the press. When his contemporaries were queried about it after his death, not one of them could recall hearing him utter the phrase.

The statement he made that comes closest is "The people like to be humbugged." But when an East Bridgeport clergyman took him to task for the remark, Barnum leaped to his own defense and insisted that he had been misquoted.

In a letter to the *Bridgeport Standard,* he wrote, "I said that the people like to be humbugged when, as in my case, there is no humbuggery except that which consists in throwing up skyrockets and issuing flaming bills and advertisements to attract public attention to shows which all acknowledge are always clean, moral, instructive, elevating and give back to their patrons in every case several times their money's worth."

Two years after Barnum's death, Thomas Ball's bronze statue was mounted on a granite base paid for by the people of Bridgeport and placed in Seaside Park. It was unveiled by one of Barnum's great-granddaughters on July 4, 1893.

The statue remains in Seaside Park till this day. Looking genial and contented, the showman gazes out over the blue-gray waters of Long Island Sound. The pencil he once held in his right hand is gone, a victim of wind, weather, or vandals, but there is a half-open memo book in his left hand.

Thomas Ball may have imagined him making notes

for another version of his autobiography, or planning a tour for General Tom Thumb, or creating another spectacle for the Greatest Show on Earth. Whatever the sculptor had in mind, he has captured P. T. Barnum doing the one thing the showman always found difficult to do in life—sitting still.

For Further Reading

If you are interested in reading more about P. T. Barnum and his career as a showman, the following books are suggested:

Culhane, John, *The American Circus*. New York: Henry Holt & Co., 1989.

Desmond, Alice Curtis, *Barnum Presents General Tom Thumb*. New York: Macmillan, 1954.

Fitzsimons, Raymund, *Barnum in London*. New York: St. Martin's Press, 1970.

Harris, Neil, *Humbug: The Art of P. T. Barnum*. Boston: Little, Brown, 1973.

Schultz, Gladys, *Jenny Lind: The Swedish Nightingale*. Philadelphia: Lippincott, 1962.

Wallace, Irving and Wallace, Amy, *The Two; a Biography*. New York: Simon & Schuster, 1978.

Index

Page numbers in italics refer to photographs.

158